Positive Failure

Alastair Arnott MSc

Printed and bound in the United Kingdom by:
4edge Ltd, 7a Eldon Way Industrial Estate, Hockley, Essex, SS5 4AD.

All 8 exam failure quotations reproduced with permission from 'F in Exams – The best Test Paper Blunders' by Richard Benson and Summersdale Publishers Ltd. £5.99 Illustrating real pupils' responses to real exam questions.

Front cover design by Luke Clift.

*'When everything goes wrong, what a joy to test your soul
and see if it has endurance and courage!'*
Nikos Kazantzakis, Zobra The Greek

Contents

It is not the critic who counts; not the man who points out how the strong man stumbles, or where the doer of deeds could have done them better. The credit belongs to the man who is actually in the arena, whose face is marred by dust and sweat and blood; who strives valiantly; who errs, who comes short again and again, because there is no effort without error and shortcoming; but who does actually strive to do the deeds; who knows great enthusiasms, the great devotions; who spends himself in a worthy cause; who at the best knows in the end the triumph of high achievement, and who at the worst, if he fails, at least fails while daring greatly, so that his place shall never be with those cold and timid souls who neither know victory nor defeat.
– Theodore Roosevelt

Excerpt from the speech "Citizenship in a Republic" delivered at the Sorbonne, in Paris, France on 23 April, 1910.

Acknowledgements

Firstly, thank you to my wife Megan for her constant patience, love and support. I also thank my family, Andrew, Kathy, Thomas and Alexandra, for their support and love, especially when I was a teenager!

I would also like to thank Glenda Bozalina-Hollingsworth and Larry Hollingsworth for their unconditional acceptance in addition to the Texas family.

Sincere thanks to my good friends Dean and Annette Lloyd-Jones and Robert and Amy Christer, for their continuous support over the years.

Thank you to Philomena Steele, head teacher of St Edmund Campion.

I want to acknowledge in particular the research and exemplary teaching style of Dr Nash Popovic, Dr Kate Hefferon and Dr Ilona Boniwell and the University of East London Positive Psychology team.

I would also like to thank Sharon, Phil and Paul Maynard, in addition, the Lisa and Dave Brine family, for being a harbour in a storm.

Thank you to Inese Nielsen for proof reading and editing. Also thank you to Andrew Young and all at Cambridge Academic Publishers. I also thank Sir Tim Brighouse.

Finally, a very special thank you to the following pupils who were the first real 'positive failure' experiment in 'The Chronicles of Narnia' production 5th and 7th November 2012:

John McErlean, Tyler Ward, Barbara Nielsen, Jessica Grady, Lauren Grady, Cassandra Porteous, Sharnni Munn, Chris Howard, Jerome Pinnock-Glasgow, Thomas Harrington, Georgina Fitzsimmons, Helen Tivnan, Ryan Wallace, Megan Storer, Sam Gardiner, Chloe Mills, Tom Hill, Helen Vlachou.

Preface

I think teenagers in their many shapes and forms are great. I believe we all have a vulnerable teenager inside us.

Something quite frightening seems to be happening. More and more, teenagers are getting it right, very early on in their school career. They are absorbing and repeating back to us the same lessons, facts and diagrams we learnt – faster.

Socially, most are connected electronically and communicate at the speed of light. They are terrified of failing, often alone, isolated and in my opinion, psychologically ill prepared for a world that is becoming increasingly volatile.

I had always dismissed failure and tried to avoid it like the plague. As the idea for positive failure grew, I observed and engaged with some tremendously successful people, one common factor they all shared was that they had all failed hard and seemed to have built up a cumulative immunity to the feelings that failure often produces. They had embraced failure as a tool for development of outstanding people and in some cases purposefully placed it at the centre of their practice.

As this topic grew and ideas began to form, incubate and re-form, I noticed patterns of failure running through everything the human race has ever done. It seems to be what we are best at!

Instrumental in the process of learning and my theory, is positive psychology. A fascinating and ever growing new branch of psychology that has much to offer the world and education. My passion lies with doing everything in my power to ensure that teenagers meet their own challenges equipped psychologically to continue to learn, adapt and progress through anything the world can throw at them.

Introduction

'One fails forward toward success.'
– Charles F. Kettering

This book attempts to conceptualise failure. In time everything will fail. It is an extremely pessimistic standpoint, however true. From the new washing machine to the sun and universe itself. I believe that failure is one of our most powerful tools of learning and development. Such an important aspect of human development deserves to be understood fully, whatever occupation or facet of life we occupy.

In this book, I present a new theory of failure and explore why it is such a tricky subject. It has turned out that the roots of failure seem to lie in our schooldays. What is the difference between the person who fails because they can't be bothered, the person who works themselves to the bone to achieve those goals and then fails? 'How to' has been done. We all know how to diet, how to get that perfect grade and how to relax. We don't need 'how to'. What has not been covered is when 'how to' fails. The obstacles that stand in our way and defeat that is inevitable in our own personal journeys, the relentless perfectionism we strive to achieve and the taboo of being seen as weak.

This book presents a deeper understanding of failure and a new theory to be applied in your own world. Failure is a natural and powerful psychological force. Without an understanding of it, we will see how it has managed to abuse, hinder and slow our development for thousands of years. Do we have a responsibility to question ourselves? I think we do and I argue that when it involves our children (indeed the progression of our race) we all will bear the consequences if we do not. We seem to be unable to get our heads around this idea. This is not a new idea and we can take comfort in the fact that it seems to almost be a human blueprint that failure has eluded and confused us for generation after generation of scientists, psychologists and heretics.

Aside from the friendships and social skills you developed, what did you learn at school? Really think about it. Dependent upon the age of the reader the result will vary. Would it fill a page? How relevant have those exams been in your life so far? How important did they seem at the time? How important did your parents, carers or guardians think those grades were? How much real world application of those grades in Maths, Science and English have you used? To understand failure, we need to go back to school.

Have you ever paused and thought about William Shakespeare as a child? I hadn't. As Ken Robinson said in one of his lectures: "Can you imagine being his English teacher?". Making up words and prancing around? I wonder how he would fare in today's school system? Would he have passed his English?

Our children are failing to learn because they haven't learnt how to fail. They are more confident, more individual and more vulnerable than they ever have been. Their self-esteem is at record levels, yet employers the world over, complain of how they are just not up to the standard required. When they don't know what to do, they crumble. Do they have the resilience necessary to secure the job or career they want? They are labelled as bright, dim, clever or stupid at younger and younger ages. The IQ test continues to be the basis for the 11+ exam in the UK and is over 100 years old. Can you imagine if medicine, technology or science still used instruments and measurements from 100 years ago? Education is relevant to the vast majority of people in the western world and it is usually compulsory in one form or another. Research has shown that whilst certain mistakes can actually kill us, in mainstream life many more of them just make us feel awful and like we want to die. This would explain why the word mortify seems to rear its head when people talk about their failures (Schulz, 2010).

I argue that the human mind is enormously elastic. Precious few pupils in school are operating anywhere near the ceiling of their ability, and through no fault of teachers, school is just not stretching our children as it should. A study by David Perkins (1985) of Harvard University has shown that after primary school, there is almost no effect of education on how well people think in daily life when they are outside their particular areas of specialism. There have been multiple advances since 1985 but it does ask the question, how useful is our current curriculum? According to David Perkins, between the ages of 11 and 16 the accurate memorisation required to pass exams produces virtually no improvement in the way young people think when they are outside the classroom or examination hall.

Thomas Edison is considered one of the most prolific inventors in history, holding 1,093 U.S patents to his name. When he was a boy his teacher told him he was too stupid to learn anything. When he set out on his own, he tried more than 9,000 experiments before he created the first successful light bulb.

Abraham Lincoln only had 5 years at school. When he grew up, he joined politics and had 12 major failures in elections before he was elected the 16th President of the United States of America. Many think that Isaac Newton was born a genius. He did very poorly in school, so poorly in fact, that his teachers despaired and couldn't find ways to improve his grades.

Beethoven's music teacher once said of him:"As a composer, he is hopeless".

All of the above people went on to do amazing things in human history. The common factor here is, they were either told they were no good at school, or got low grades. Yet in the world of education, we are so fixated with predicting children's success based on tests that they take when they are under 11 years old.

We assume that qualifications will put us in a better position to work, get a better job, earn more money and be happier. Research has shown that academia, just like the economy has inflated (Robinson, 2001). This is a sociological problem. Grades seem to have been devalued. We seem to have spent 100 years going round in circles in education.

We are one of the most depressed generations to inhabit the earth. Studies have shown that we are consuming more anti-depressants and anti-anxiety medication than ever before (Brown, 2010). Something here is failing. We seem to have more possessions, more security and more technology than we have ever had. Yet we are still unhappy?

Around half of our school children in the UK, according to exam results are failures. It seems clear that many of the educational practices and policies which inform our teenagers learning have been made obsolete by new discoveries. Research has shown that the educational methods we have been using over the past 70 years are just not working (Resnick, 1999). Isn't it the kind of learning you are practicing that it is important not the subject matter you are practicing on? We can all remember those great teachers we had and how we seem to recall much easier the teachings of these great people. Research shows that the specific teachers you have and how they teach matters a great deal more than the policies or procedures that a school adopts (William, 2007). We know what we need as a race, we want young people who can critique, integrate, elaborate, challenge and create, however, research has shown that what we do not need, and in some cases currently have, are young people who are nervous and timid when it comes to knowledge (Gilbert, 2005).

Surely, we should be focusing on enhancing students overall capacities and their motivation to learn as opposed to putting them through a quality control subject system that often doesn't link and amalgamate. I propose that education should be targeted at awakening a person's mind to the consciousness of its own power by bringing it into contact with daily experience, cultivating by suitable exercise and failure, its faculties of observation, perception, reflection, judgement and reasoning aiding children to gain clear and accurate ideas of their own. I argue that in this 'Google' age, facts are not what our young people need. Students do not arrive at secondary school aged 11 with all the answers and the best grades. They arrive ready to succeed when they actually should arrive ready to fail. We have put in place a dazzling miasma of systems and procedures to ensure that pupils do not fail. The puzzling notion to me in this educational concoction is that many of us know the answer. We want adventurous, inquisitive, systematic and imaginative thinking, resilient, independent, successful, happy, non-defensive empathetic pupils to leave school and venture forth into our world. Over 15 years of research by Costa and Kallick (2000), Perkins, Jay & Tishman (1993), Ritchart (2002), Claxton's (2008) and Gilbert (2005) supports this. I argue that these qualities will surface much faster and easier if we embrace and use failure rather than choking pupils with success.

Failing hurts. It is highly unpleasant and in a perfect world it wouldn't exist. Then again a perfect world would be quite frightening in itself. Biswas-Diener (2012) describes how failure carries with it a temporary psychological sting. I argue that there must be a way to harness the very technique of failure and use it positively.

The Theory of Positive Failure

Isn't positive failure an oxymoron? Could failure be positive?

I introduce the theory of positive and negative failure. Positive failure in its simplest form is a dose of failure that is similar to a vaccination process. The process of vaccination is not pleasant. I argue that the theory of positive failure mirrors the patterns of Edward Genner's smallpox vaccine and functions within the same paradigm.

In a world of mandatory success, I argue that success can breed contempt and *positive failure* breeds progression. To distinguish between the two types of failure, I offer this definition:

Positive failure: *is failure after appropriate investment that leads to further learning or development.*

Negative failure: *is failure after inappropriate investment that stunts further progress or development.*

Conducive to positive failure are appropriately supportive and forgiving relationships in an unforgiving environment. The more realistic and tangible the challenge or standard, the more likely it is for positive failure to occur.

I argue that negative failure adversely effects self-esteem and resilience. Unlike negative failure, positive failure can increase motivation and resilience. It does not adversely affect self-esteem, but strengthens and builds it. For positive failure to yield the best results, I suggest the following preconditions are important:

Preconditions for positive failure: *acceptance of one's own vulnerability, having a growth mindset and embracing imperfection.*

Preconditions for negative failure: *defiance of one's own vulnerability, having a fixed mindset and embracing perfectionism.*

Positive failure is the spark that cultivates practical wisdom and lends itself to operating in the master virtue of resilience which we will explore later.

SCHOOL EXAM QUESTION:
1. What is a network?
Answer: When you chat to people you don't like to try and get a job.

Positive Failure

Chapter **One**
Failing to Learn

'Try again. Fail again. Fail better.'
– Samuel Beckett

The Current Situation of Learning

Although many young people live happy lives and relish their schooldays, an alarming majority are not so fortunate. Emotional problems such as anxiety and depression are up in Britain and research is showing that these issues are being taken forward into adulthood (Collinshaw, 2004, Seligman, 2011 & McCulloch, 2007). This pattern is mirrored across the globe; children's well-being worldwide is a cause for concern.

As a society, we in the west have very high expectations. Through the media and schools we suggest that responsibility, independence, academic achievement, ambition to raise a stable family, looking great, being fit, and earning large quantities of money are all valued. These messages are also beamed to us through our contact with screens. Through the media these messages are injected directly into people's psyche. I argue that we are not giving children anything like the means to achieve these high expectations. Why, in fact, for the vast majority, are we making it near impossible for children to achieve them? Why are our children so frightened of failure? I argue that it has a lot to do with impressing people. Studies have shown that there are three and four year olds who arrive at school utterly convinced that it is their job to impress their teachers, parents and society as a whole (Smiley and Dweck, 1994).

I argue that many children have been socialised into subscribing to the notion that looking great and performing well is more important than exploring, more important than hypothesizing, more important than experimenting and more important than failing. In fact, Smiley and Dweck (1994) found that certain toddlers firmly believe they never make any mistakes at all. Stress is what happens when the demands made on you exceed the resources you have to meet them. Do our children have the adequate resources to meet present and future challenges? Under the pressure of aiming for our prized values, many people feel obliged to try and manage their feelings rather than focus on the demands themselves, this can increase, and cause desperate and vivid attempts to avoid self-criticism. It has been suggested that all students be screened for psychological vulnerability. I argue that generally, there is nothing wrong with our children. What is wrong here is the system, and to find the true cause of how failure has been side stepped on the road to success and what we can do to harness its colossal power, we need to explore why, psychologically speaking, schools seem to have been beyond question for thousands of years. The use of positive failure is an untapped natural resource that is a core ingredient of great learning.

In the UK, half of all young people are failing at the qualifications game. Now, just hold on a second. This cannot be the individual child's fault, the deprived area, the problem parents or a lack of effort/ability. This is a structural and systematic issue.

More groups of young people are opting out of challenges to protect their self-worth. They are not allowed to fail. It is better not to try, than try and fail. Several pupils now firmly believe that you have to know the answer before you ask the question. In one UK study over a school year, the average student generated question is one per student, per month (Dillon, 1990). Once you leave school the plan is, you go to work. The very word 'work' does not evoke the happiest of times. I argue that hard work has been sub-culturally embedded as punishment rather than fulfilment, reward and an area of happiness. I argue that work can and ought to be a place where we experience positive emotions. In one study, it was found that teachers often experience optimal experiences and nearly all of these were when engaged with children (Delle Fave, 2003).

SCHOOL EXAM QUESTION:
2. Explain the word 'Genome'.
Answer: It is an abbreviation of the two words: Gender and Gnome.

The Biological Roots of Failure and
'The Failure Heterodoxy'

If you compare humans with all other animals, there is a striking difference. Human beings are born in an immature, vulnerable, and helpless state. This state enables children to tune into their environment, learn language and fail, often. This is how we have learnt successfully and evolved over thousands of years, through failure.

There are key actions human beings can engage in that will aid learning, one of which being failure. However, losing is not fun. Failing hurts. This was beneficial for our ancestors and, in the context of early mankind, the failure to catch an animal that has been hunted, led to a far more intense emotional experience than catching and killing the same animal. There is a link here to motivation. Those who experienced loss or failure were strongly motivated to work harder to avoid loss. Indeed those who did not experience intense emotions in response to failure or loss were not motivated to work hard, avoided loss, and probably then experienced multiple losses resulting in them dying out. This is still true today, as cave men and women, when we loose something, it hurts more than acquiring something. Alan Carr (2004) believes that this same paradigm is still present today and very much alive, for example losing £/$50 is not levelled out by the satisfaction of earning £/$50.

We are not nearly as good at absorbing and reflecting on positive events as we are at analysing bad events. This is of course a survival technique. Those of our ancestors who spent time sunbathing instead of fortifying their homes against dinosaurs did not survive. When everything is going well, we are at our most relaxed and docile. Maybe that is a good metaphor for the position our society finds ourselves now? The going is so good that maybe we believe that we don't need failure. History has taught us that this approach leads to a dead end; the world is flat – right? I argue that in our own genetic blueprint, we are designed to accept that failure is evident in learning.

We often imagine failure when we are designing or creating something new. Imagination is one of our species great gifts and we differ from our closest genetic relatives in having extensively enlarged frontal lobes, and research has shown that these control our focus, essentially meaning we can simulate experiences and future tasks without using our muscles at all (Goldberg, 2001). Newtonian law was focused on a purely logical and scientific sense of reason, for example, the phrase: *I'll believe it when I see it.* In modern times, the opposite seems to resonate more: *I'll see it when I believe it.* The most useful learning seems to happen when we combine imagination and logic. Studies have shown that this produces the best results as far as learning and intelligence go (Bannerman *et al*, 2006, and Claxton, 2006).

When planning for something we try and think out the possible areas where it could go wrong, we complete risk assessments and we test. Yet, failure always seems to come at us from out of nowhere. Extensive research has shown that having it too good, is an obstacle to happiness itself and the people who can re-adapt after both the good and bad times are the ones who will survive. (Zahavi and Zahavi *et al*, 1997, Buss, 2000, Friedrick and Lowenstein, 1999). We do have it relatively good compared to other periods in history, and in education we seem to be obsessed with success. We need to be careful.

We seem to struggle with the constant comparison of ourselves with others. We seem to spend a disproportionate amount of time doing this. The big comparison between modern day and civilisations in the past is our access to the media. Through the media, we now have access to perverted and elitist comparisons such as excellence in physical attractiveness, excellence in work and the ideal human relationships. We are unwittingly leading our psychologically vulnerable teenagers into a world of comparisons with the successful elite where no one fails...ever. I am happy knowing that I don't, or ever will, look as attractive as the latest celebrity supermodel, yet multiple product advertising tells me that if I work harder, buy this or that, it is achievable and I should follow my dream. As we shall see later that often the 'dream' actually leads to a promiscuous miasma of negativity and dissatisfaction. I argue that in most cases the standards teenagers set themselves through school are either unrealistic and unattainable, so low it is painful to listen to, or are just confused about where they want to go. With age and experience we seem to become more content with accepting what we have. Maybe if we psychologically knew ourselves better at school when we were teenagers, we could have made better decisions. Aiming high is a wonderful aspiration and working hard to achieve is great. However, education continues to nurture the belief that we can all be number 1 and the very best. I argue that we are not equally gifted, we are not equally talented, we are not all the same, by the numbers very definition, and we cannot all be number one. Above all, we are not perfect.

I argue that one of the vital things that some parents and teachers do wrong, is prematurely rescue their children from learning challenges. Children are naturally resilient. Babies in particular are incredibly resilient. For example, if we take the complex task of learning to walk. They will fail, over and over, looking very silly whilst failing. They don't worry about looking stupid, they want to learn to walk, and if that takes falling over or 'failing' dozens of times - so be it. The problem occurs when parents or teachers inadvertently lead our children to believe that mistakes whilst learning are something that it is right to be upset about, and I believe that that is exactly what is happening in schools in western society.

Research on key theories of capital and symbolic power, introduces the idea of heterodoxy as the part of a society or class that is beyond question, undiscussed and undisputed, the unquestioning values of a society (Bourdieu's, 1992). These values can be good. It is unquestioned that stealing is wrong and rightly so. However, could it be that failure has maintained a stealthy heterodoxy due to the emotional attachment to failure that we seem to have and the negative affect of comparing oneself to others? By setting a pattern that mistakes and failure are negative – have we created a false doctrine? An unquestioning attitude, that failure is negative and to be avoided completely? I believe so. The heterodoxy around failure goes against everything we have achieved thus far in human progression, not only it is getting in the way of our evolution, I argue that it is forcing us *backwards* in terms of intelligence.

I argue that failure itself can be positive and, in the right circumstances, can be one of the key drivers of human development and evolution. I would argue that it is essential that children fail. If we protect children from failure we weaken their self-esteem and do not improve it. We may as well humiliate, pacify, thwart them and then abandon them. Indeed research has shown that without failure we can weaken self-esteem (Seligman, 2003).For some bizarre reason we seem to regard our default human state as being correct or getting it right. When we slip up, it leaves us feeling stupid, ashamed, it doesn't happen often, right? It is completely the opposite. Our natural human default is failure. We are on this planet for a short while and then our organs will fail and we will die. We make thousands, maybe millions of mistakes and we fail our way forward as we have done for thousands of years. If we look back through history, I believe that the mistakes and failures of mankind are far more interesting than our successes. Research has shown that twelve hundred years before Rene Descartes penned his famous 'I think therefore I am', the philosopher and theologian Saint Augustine wrote 'fallor ergo sum' - I err therefore I am (Bettenson, 2003). We are aware that error, failure and being wrong are central to our development. We just aren't using them anywhere near as much as we should....yet.

SCHOOL EXAM QUESTION:
3. What were Jesus's closest group of followers known as?
Answer: The 12 decibels.

The History of Learning

We know that learning is fluid, incomplete and contentious. It is a fact that people are still arguing over what Aristotle wrote and what he meant by it. Studies on ancient philosophy have shown that Aristotle never tried to explain a fully worked out philosophy. He often took the viewpoint of experimenting with different assumptions and different viewpoints. Socrates would say anything and often challenge pupils own, taken for granted beliefs (Hadot, 2002). Both saw knowledge not as a grade, result or exam paper in itself, but as a resource for progress. Wisdom in this sense seems to me to be a combination of situational, problem and person specific interventions and provocations, not facts and repetitions of truth repeated back to them in a pressurised situation such as in an exam hall.

I argue that our sense of what school is and what it should be is driven by dead metaphors that are part of the failure heterodoxy. These images are so engrained in our society that they drive our misconceptions unconsciously and with great cost to our children, and it's not acceptable. 4000 years ago both in China and the Middle East, a specific model for the education of children was developed based around the teachings required for priesthood. The priests talked to god and it was important that this was conveyed accurately and with a sense of an unquestioning attitude. This paradigm driven teaching and learning, based on the unquestioning authority of a few high status initiatives, has been mirrored throughout history. As we moved into the medieval age teachers, tutors and professors even adopted a similar clothing style to priests.

The precise memorisation of knowledge was the way forward. Full and completely qualified teachers in Geometry, Latin, Arithmetic and Grammar dispensed this knowledge. They then tested their students and decided their grade. The image of school as a monastery persists up to present day. The classroom of the first recorded civilization on earth in the Persian Gulf, the Mesopotamia in 2500 BC would be frighteningly similar to the British or American student of present day.

With the influx of the industrial revolution, education in the nineteenth century education changed from being an induction into power for the upper classes to an entitlement for the masses. A likening of schools to the factory metaphor was conceived by Hermine H Marshall (1990) of San Francisco State University who has completed over a decade of monographs devoted to the difference between learning and work environments. Guy Claxton (2008) in ʻ*Whatʼs the Point of School?*ʼ comments on the outcome of the research:

> "*Knowledge can be standardised, installed in manuals called ʻtext-booksʼ and chopped up into different sized bits – syllabuses, topics, schemes of work and eventually the content of individual lessons – that can be bolted on, as it were, to students minds bit by bit. Harder or more advanced components could only be fixed on successfully if the easier or earlier ones were securely attached already. Teachers may have a sense of the big picture but students have no more need of the blueprint than does a radio. As on the production line, quality control is essential, the ʻproductsʼ are regularly tested and graded to make sure that the operation has been successful. If they are found to be faulty, it is usually because they are intrinsically so – ʻlow abilityʼ or ʻlazyʼ. Quality control requires considerable numbers of students to be graded as ʻsecondsʼ or ʻrejectsʼ but recently it has been thought that this kind of language can damage studentsʼ self-esteem, so confusing forms of language have been developed that mask the continuing quality control operation. Around half of the products are regularly rejected after ten years of educational processing.*" (P51-52).

The mass production of literate, honest, punctual and dutiful workers had merit and currency in the industrial revolution. This metaphor is not only dead but is still very much functioning in a complete heterodoxy in todayʼs state primary and secondary schools. Positive and negative failures have been around pretty much since the dawn of man. We fully recognise that we are not perfect. Many religious traditions include a ritual for penitence, confession and purification. We do recognise that we all make mistakes and that nobody is perfect. We also recognise that failure is something that happens to everyone. So why are we so obsessed with perfection?

Are Schools Failing?

Schools across the world are obsessed with success, and for good reason. Of course we want our children to achieve; we also want our children to be real world learners. In this book I primarily examine the British and American education systems. Slightly different versions of the same system are in place all over the English speaking world and some, in the non-English speaking world.

Any manufacturer who consistently produced over 50% of rejects would not stay in business for long. Research has shown that in the UK schools are dramatically failing. 350,000 pupils fail to make the GCSE (main benchmark of British academia, taken at 16) grade C in English, Maths and Science (Claxton, 2008). There is a recent plan to scrap the GCSE entirely; then again there is often a political plan to change assessment to produce more success. There is a strong rumour that British industry has lost faith in the GCSE exams, because so many young people with GCSE passes are unable to function adequately in the workplace. It is thought that one in three businesses are being forced to send staff (many of them graduates) for additional lessons in literacy and numeracy.

There does exist a stereotypical view on the relation between ability and effort and it seems to be that, there isn't one. Therefore, someone who exerts more effort is only doing so in order to make up for their lack of ability. This causes psychological problems. Some American and British students do not see a rational reason why they should put forth extra effort into their academic studies because it seems quite futile. Studies show that according to this logic, the more effort a student invests into a task, the more they are affirming that they are inherently unintelligent so: the harder it is, the more stupid you are (Holloway, 1988). Japanese students are taught to believe that their whole life, not just their academic future, relies directly upon the amount of work they put into their studies. As a result, the motivation to succeed is not to get good grades, to get money or rewards from their parents, or for someone else to tell them they are intelligent. Their motivation has much more to do with the drive to a certain life goal or ideal. It is therefore, intrinsic motivation. This can obviously come at a cost, and Japanese school students have a frighteningly high suicide rate. There must be a middle ground here.

Curriculum

In ancient times Plato developed the *timeless verities* view of an educational curriculum. His view was that through studying the best knowledge, students' minds would become formatted along the same lines. The more abstract and pure the knowledge studied, the better it would develop and polish the students powers of abstract reasoning. Plato thought this would be the most valuable form of intelligence in future leaders of society.

Do we still need this paradigm? The very content of the curriculum is as unquestioned as failure in state schools. Professor Richard Aldrich (2008) the UK's foremost historian of education asked the question, How has the curriculum, [like the IQ test] endured years of educational reform? The 1904 Secondary School Regulations required schools to teach English, Maths, Science, History, Geography, a foreign language, drawing, physical exercise and manual work/housewifery. The list of subjects in the 1988 National Curriculum was identical bar the last category and music was added. So in our rapidly changing world, in our world that is changing at a pace that is so fast it has never been experienced before, children in schools in England are following much the same curriculum as they were at the end of the nineteenth century. It seems there has been very little education structural progression. Has it made our children any more confident at deducing, exploring or hypothesising? In simpler societies the classroom was normal life itself. The adults and elders going about their business acted as informal guides and role models and the children watched, copied and took small but increasingly responsible parts in normal life, making non-catastrophic failures. This type of learning is downright messy, and it works. Rather than focusing on impressing high status people and regurgitation, the apprentice model focused on the development of skills, attributes and people failed. It is well known amongst outstanding practitioners in teaching and learning that the best type of learning is to just do it. Rather than talk about it, explain it or guess about it. To *do it* takes courage and if you are attempting it for the first time, then you will probably fail.

What is Intelligence? I believe that part of Intelligence is working to figure things out, trying different strategies until a workable solution is found and that means, getting it wrong. These are the questions we need to be asking ourselves as our children grow and learn. Research has shown that students who have over an extended period of time been treated as if they are intelligent actually do become so. If they are taught difficult and demanding content, the high expectations are in place, they are expected to explain and find connections as well as memorise and repeat – then these pupils will learn more and learn faster (Resnick, 1999). Crucially, it seems they will also be able to overcome instances of failure.

It is clear we seem to have a structural problem in secondary education. As educators we seem very keen on short-term interventions. It has been proven by research conducted by a Harvard Professor that short-term interventions are not useful and tend to enhance test-manship more than general cognitive efficiency and that they diminish over time (Perkins, 1985). The impact that is needed here is on the front line, in the life of the classrooms and playgrounds, an understanding of positive failure. An interesting new assessment procedure has been developed where researchers found that young people's ability to stay focused and engaged with a task and not give up, predicted their performance on school tests twice as well as their IQ. Self- discipline also predicted which students would improve their grades over the course of the year while IQ did not (Duckworth and Seligman, 2005). IQ seems to me to be an assumption of a measure for intelligence rather than a measure in itself.

There have been suggestions recently that failure is so demoralising and painful for youngsters that their poor performance has to be rebranded as *deferred success* or *nearly*. Very few exam candidates actually fail these days. Employers have been found to send employees to basic literacy, numeracy and interpersonal skills classes because they have passed, because they have succeeded at school and their success does not translate into the real world.

It is common knowledge that it is estimated technology is going to overtake us. It is rumoured that by 2029 computers will equal us in brainpower, they will be able to recite the periodic table under pressurised situations much faster than you and me. For 4,000 years school has been based on our crude understanding of how our brains work. In the last thirty years new knowledge opened up new questions, new answers and can, perhaps, be the scientific basis of a new national curriculum. A new curriculum is intimidating and experiments of new 'stuff' on children are risky. I ask, what is more frightening, trying new ideas and curricula, or continuing to put up with the same curriculum that has partly led to half of British school children to fail, and worse, believing that they themselves are failures as they progress into adult life. In a medical sense, we would never dream of dispensing untested drugs into the general public, yet schools routinely invest in educational and organisational improvement programs where the only evidence that they work comes from their own promotion. People's lives may be affected with the same severity as using untested drugs.

SCHOOL EXAM QUESTION:
4. What is conditional probability?
Answer: Maybe; maybe not.

Manipulating Grades

Through governments putting pressure on schools and head teachers to achieve results the pressure on schools is building. A six-year-old is not half a 12-year-old. There have been reports that the specialist schools and academies trust drafted a plan with the DfES to encourage Universities to establish links with the pre-teen students who excel in their year 6 (11-year-olds) tests. One chairman is convinced that bright 11-year-olds should achieve three As at A level and want secondary school heads to be made accountable if those students don't make it. This takes no account of new learning, new motivation, new effort and new challenges.

Head teachers and teachers are not the only ones who may feel they have to manipulate data, grades, results and tests under the pressure to be seen as 'succeeding'. Children aren't stupid and many find it hard to resist the temptation to do a little, or a lot downloading from the Internet if the pressure on results is high. When the pressure on results is high, people will find ways of achieving those results. Cheating is on the rise and even in school exams blatant cheating is on the rise, a huge proportion of school pupils are caught every year trying to smuggle their mobile phones into examination halls across the country.

The pressure on educationalists is increasing on almost a weekly basis. Research has shown that, the sanctions attached to failure are now so huge that many teachers feel drilling multiple choice questions is what they have to do to ensure that targets and grade expectations are met (Williams, 2006). A huge amount is at stake. Maybe the answer is to remove the sanctions and accept that failure is evident in learning process?

My Child is *'Low Ability'*?

'Failure is an event, never a person.'
– William D. Brown

I argue that administrating labels is dangerous in any organisation. How we are seen and classed at school when we are at one of our most vulnerable ages (our teens) can have a substantial effect on us. If we are treated like we are 'clever' or 'stupid', often we believe it for a disproportionate amount of time. The way children see themselves has been shown by research to be heavily influenced by the perceptions of others (Cole, Maxwell & Martin, 1997). In education, it brands us and leaves a scar that often leaves feelings of inadequacy, yet on paper we are a success. Did you feel ready for the real world when you left school? Getting it right or getting it wrong can affect our image of ourselves sometimes for our entire lives. We seem to have confused Intelligence with academic skill. Those children who perform at a lower standard in the academic subjects (often English and Maths) are often labelled as less able. Academic ability is important. However we seem to be fixated upon this to the point that we exclude other subjects. This gives a distorted and confusing representation of the future to our students.

I speculate that any parent would be shocked at hearing the words, 'I am sorry but your child is stupid.' What does the phrase 'low ability' actually mean? Does it mean stupid? How many of us were given up on by teachers and school and have gone on to achieve tremendous feats of intelligence and progress? Phrases like 'low ability' and 'lazy' are crude and unhelpful. This is part of the problem. The fatal idea that education is a game at which a large proportion of young people are bound to fail is antiquated, untrue and unacceptable. Once a child is labelled low ability, it can be tempting to pity and pour sympathy over them, working with the bottom set, one can find it all too easy to lower the standard for the entire class. Studies have shown that unsolicited offers of help and too much sympathy from teachers can lead to students attributing their academic setbacks to low ability (Graham, 1991). After all what is the point in trying if you're stupid? You're only going to fail.

In the UK and USA we have a category of students called *gifted and talented/able*. Over the world they are called the *cream, the top set* and *1st class*, amongst others. There is a school of thought that labelling students *gifted and talented* may benefit from the Pygmalion or self–fulfilling prophecy idea, which is that; by labelling them as great they may become great. However, they may also suffer from the weight of expectation and pressure at being officially registered as 'bright' therefore making them a more anxious and conservative learner. Those who don't make it onto the list may of course suffer from a reverse Pygmalion effect and stand less chance of pushing their way forward if they happen to be a late developer. In a recent study, it was shown that the label gifted and talented as was often taken as meaning, possessing inherent, all round, high ability. The label in reality is often given to children who have developed particular social and learning skills such as eye contact, smiling and asking questions from what was just said by the teacher (Balchin, 2008).

There exists still a huge allocated budget for working with the *gifted and talented*, shouldn't that mean working with all children, giving as many children as possible as many learning opportunities? Or does that mean that just because a child didn't pass their English or Maths they are therefore denied these opportunities? The old fashioned teaching of grammar has also been proven to be ineffective. Research from the University of York in 2005, found no evidence that teaching the parts of speech, noun phrases, relative clauses and so on, helped 5- to 16-year-olds improve the quality of their writing (Andrews and Torgerson, *et al* 2006).

I argue that what students are doing as they dissect the proof of Pythagoras theorem and or the theory of natural selection is now completely different from what Pythagoras and Darwin were doing when they were wandering, watching, and deducing for the first time. Whilst these theories are relevant, I am sure Darwin did not wish his own theory to be regurgitated for a grade. At the same time, it is important and there is value in mastering the basics. I argue that both students and teachers seem to be impatient with learning processes that don't yield results quickly and this makes us dumb down, shorten and simplify processes at secondary level.

For a very long time Intelligence was viewed as a general, central vat of non-specific mental competence that determined your course of action in daily life. If you were 'bright' your brightness would go with you into your geography lesson. Being 'dim' stayed with you in the same way that your DNA stayed with you. I believe that this mindset has led many people in education to focus far more on what can't be changed about a young person's intelligence than what can. Fixed ability seems to have a chokehold over people's attitudes about intelligence and particularly in state education. Dawkins (1996) along with Blackmore (1999) call this focus on fixed ability a *'meme'*: a tenacious, self-replicating idea.

The older children get the more expensive their education. Can everyone do a PhD? What would happen if we did? We, human beings, also are very fond of everything in its rightful place, we make judgements and we attribute particular characteristics to other people on information that is often found lacking. For example, so if someone yawns in a lesson it must mean that they think it is boring. If they fail an exam then they are not bright. This tendency is so ubiquitous; psychologist Philip Tetlock (1985) gave it its own name: *fundamental attribution error*. We all do it to greater or lesser degrees, and it is the basis of much comedy. Teachers also have a colossal amount of names, numbers and grades to deal with on a day-to-day basis. The need to impose some sort of order on this setting of mass personalities and interactions is completely understandable.

Indeed, through my own experience, it is nigh impossible to report on children's progress without using data or some sort of classification. It is much easier to say; 'Jessica is a bright child' or 'Tyler is a little terror.' Despite the reasons for this fixed ability attitude. The real issue with these judgments is, once made, are hardly ever taken back. For example, if the 'clever child' makes a mistake then they are having a bad day, or not fulfilling their potential. The over achieving lower ability student, however, is reported back to that it must have been a surge of effort as opposed to an increase in ability. I argue that your intelligence is not fixed. This is explored in much more detail later. This kind of labelling has destroyed some adult's sense of achievement and how they see themselves. Fixed intelligence is at the centre of our education systems.

It was thought for a long time that bright students learned faster, were the first to finish and generally found learning easier than average or dim people. They certainly didn't make mistakes and this fed the failure heterodoxy. When someone was making mistakes, it could be interpreted that they were close to the ceiling of their intelligence. I argue that this is *profoundly* mistaken. The IQ test was used as evidence for the 11+ exam which sorted children into different kinds of education on the form of their intelligence. Richardson (1999) describes the Spens report of 1983, in which he argued that it is possible at a very early age to predict with accuracy the ultimate level of a child's intellectual capabilities, thus the foundations of the failure heterodoxy. In line with the growth mindset approach, I argue that this is foolish. The idea of fixed intelligence is a massive heterodoxy and has been so toxic it has damaged a generation of learner's confidence, self-esteem and self-efficacy. It continues to damage generation after generation.

Another phrase that is often used in education the world over is *fulfilling your potential*. If this is meant in the form that we should not to underestimate how good someone could be, it seems honourable. However, when it is measured, dissected and used to predict grades and push children, it no longer serves its purpose. How would we feel if, not only were we told our child was low ability but also had little potential? When we really think about it, I argue that the phrase 'fulfilling your potential' does not make sense. How do students know when they have fulfilled it? How does anyone? Is it an endless futile journey for achievement? One professor at Queensland University believes that 'it is a fundamental human right in itself to decline the invitation to fulfil your potential'. (McWilliam, 2002).

The growth mindset theory coined by Carol Dweck, explains how the brain is like a muscle. She suggests to look for ways every young person's mind can be stretched and strengthened rather than to label and sort them, in terms of a hypothetical amount of brain power that will not change over time. I argue that this is what good teachers have been doing for generations. Research has shown that if you label a child as 'not bright', it often leads many young people to decide to not try and solve problems that they feel are difficult (Dweck, 2007 and Resnick, 1999). I would add, maybe this is because they are afraid of failing. There seems to be a completely false belief that if one struggles then you are reaching the limit of your intelligence. I argue that belief in any ability label, if you believe it to be valid and fixed, has the effect of weakening commitment and effort when facing difficult tasks. In my experience students who are labelled 'bright or intelligent' hide their failures and difficulties away and when/if found out, experience shame and guilt. Students who are praised and told they are bright often come to associate their brightness with easy success. So when the going gets tough or if they start to fail, it is evidence that they are not as bright as they thought.

Research has proven that 'bright' girls are especially prone to experience psychological and/or emotional distress when confronted by something they don't immediately know how to do (Dweck, 2007). Indeed, many successful people are badly affected by their first experience of real [negative] failure whenever it arrives, and arrive it will. It's not just that they didn't get the result they wanted or expected; they may suffer a full blown psychological crisis as they may have never really failed in school before. Surely we should be instilling the notion and the one most important lesson of all, shouldn't we all know what to do when we don't know what to do?

Focusing on and improving pupils levels of psychological resilience seems to be something that many schools struggle with. I argue that very rarely are children coached effectively and/or systematically in the psychological skills that will enable them to meet the demands of real life with confidence. Several studies by The University of Bristol have shown that students' perceptions of their own effectiveness and confidence as learners drop significantly from KS2 to KS3. 13 year olds see themselves as less resilient, less resourceful, less curious and less good at teamwork than do 9 year olds. The New Economics foundation report publicised a report in 2004 which found a dramatic drop in young people's ability to be curious and engage in challenging and absorbing activities within a matter of weeks after attending secondary school. Even successful students are failing to learn how to learn for themselves. There seems to be a large base of evidence that many successful students quickly become frightened, nervous, worried and insecure when confronted with real problems they cannot immediately solve.

Chapter **Two**
Failing to Fail

'Success is going from failure to failure without a loss of enthusiasm.'
– Winston Churchill

It's How You Feel that Counts?

It seems that by avoiding failure we compound and feed negative traits, attributes and habits that cause us distress, pain and suffering. We fail to fail. Studies show that we are the most medicated, addicted, materialistic and depressed generation so far in human evolution (Brown 2010). We have also placed a large importance on how we feel in the moment. It is now very important to be happy. The media targets this notion with such methods as the ever-growing sexualisation of our children. To explore this more we need to take a closer look at self-esteem.

Self-esteem is the skill of successfully using ones competencies and abilities to reach personal goals. Low self-esteem occurs when people are neglected and belittled, or when they feel unable to get what they want. When children cannot see that it is their *interpretation* of, and not the fact of, failure that is affecting their feelings, their learning is going to be fragile and brittle. When teachers try to hide failure or remove the difficulty of learning to avoid 'damaging the students feelings' it can cause difficulty. When they accept the fixed view of intelligence, fixed view of ability, and that failure undermines self-esteem, it is not surprising that many teachers either mark in green pen because apparently, red effects the students' feelings too much. They are also told to tone down feedback. I argue that real self-esteem is born from the pride of having managed to overcome difficulty by yourself. This process includes failure. Nobody ever got fitter by avoiding exercise. Research shows that it is the students who are most protected from challenges and frustrations of learning that are the most exposed.

An intervention that encourages students to feel good about themselves regardless of work will remove the reason to work hard, resulting in poorer performance. High self-esteem is not the 'magic pill' for learning that it is made out to be and Carol Craig, CEO of the Centre for Confidence and Well-being, explains how people with a low self-esteem are more likely to harm themselves; but people with a higher self-esteem are more likely to harm others around them and society. Indeed it seems that many aggressive young men turn out to have a high, but fragile sense of self-esteem. There seems to be a murky paradigm that the educational world came to agree that its overriding priority was to make children feel good about themselves.

No one should feel inferior to anyone else and certainly not a failure, nothing must be too difficult. The uncomfortable truth that little of value is achieved without effort was outlawed. I argue that learning should be frustrating, if one places high value and sanctions on self-esteem in learning then this makes one lower the challenge. We have undoubtedly lowered the challenge.

The Self-Esteem Movement

America fully embraced the concept of self-esteem in the 1970s. Educational and child-rearing practices throughout the USA in the past 20 years have tried to protect and foster self-esteem. Unsuccessfully. One could speculate that self-esteem was embraced so vigorously because of the Second World War, and so much awful loss.

The failure of the self-esteem movement in American education illustrates the vulnerability of the field of psychology to inspiring but wrong-headed ideas. This is fine; as long as we recognise that some of them are wrong, and do something about it. Roy Baumeister *et al* (2003) decided that he would attempt to provide the psychological evidence needed to support the importance of self-esteem in learning. His research not only showed that self-esteem was irrelevant to academic success, it also showed that those with high self-esteem were more likely to be a problem for society than those with low self-esteem. His research showed that those who thought very well of themselves were more likely to be aggressive or indulge in risky behaviours. He also found that deliberate attempts to boost self-esteem have *no* positive effect on performance and sometimes can make it worse. Much of this evidence has been openly and publicly ignored in the USA. One author explained how self-esteem is woven into American tradition and is both definitive and constraining. Questioning self-esteem in this context would mean questioning who you were as an American (Slater, 2002).

Coming to the conclusion that we have failed can be traumatic. It often also necessitates finding a replacement belief, something else becomes the truth. What's more we are often quick to rubbish the old belief as if we never took it seriously at all. I suggest that if we are unwilling to admit this, then our belief will stay resolute and maybe – wrong?

Research has shown that there seems to be a misconception that raising self-esteem will protect youngsters from various social ills and improve their academic grades, some teachers in American and British schools have given pupils huge amounts of unwarranted praise, protected them from criticism, competition and involved them in activities where they feel 'special' and almost always win (Twenge, 2006 & Sykes, 1996). I argue that you may as well be feeding the monster. Of course, children need rescuing from real danger, but we can help their learning by not sailing in and saving them too soon. Research has shown that we can also transmit our over anxious discomfort with making mistakes to our children making them less resilient (Kagen, 1994).

Emphasising how the child feels in the moment, and making this more important than the learning, can undermine academic performance. Sadly these results are also beginning to appear in the UK and through programs like SEAL (social and emotional aspects of learning); the UK is beginning to head down a similar path. The government's response to this in the UK has been tougher standards. It poses the question from an educational point of view: has the failure of the self-esteem revolution contributed to the economic downturn? People don't seem to be getting paid for feeling 'special'. The decline in academic standards and basic literacy and numeracy is a serious problem for American employers. Even a decade ago it was estimated that American employers spend around $30 billion a year training their employees in basic skills. Studies have shown that employers complain that young employees want to get on quickly and make lots of money, however are uninterested in working their way up through an organisation or putting in real effort. They seem to be more sensitive and certainly do not like being corrected (Twenge, 2006). This does not sound to me like a good employee.

The media and popular culture supports the self-esteem revolution. Why wouldn't they? There is a lot of money to be made out of teenagers who want to feel good at any cost. It is now incredibly popular to be individual and ignore society's rules and regulations. How you feel is now paramount. Facebook is a good illustration of this. The website currently has more than 800 million active users worldwide and rising. Each user is encouraged to set a "status" often, of how they are feeling.

Emotional Intelligence Abuse

Emotional intelligence has its place and is important; studies show that emotionality is a co-operative and synergistic function that works with our powers of reasoning and cognition (Maslow, 1965 & 1987). I am convinced that at some level emotional states do influence cognition. Research by Gray, Braver & Raichle (2002) has shown that emotional states selectively influenced cognition related neural activity in the lateral prefrontal cortex. Gardener (1980) argued that we needed to broaden our view of intelligence. Gardener's work had considerable impact on two academic psychologists, John Mayer and Peter Salovey (1990). They published a paper called *Emotional Intelligence*. Their basic premise was that emotions could *serve* rationality rather than *interfere* with it.

This as it may be, through a process of pseudoscience, has been abused. In this case emotional intelligence was used as the scientific grounding for boosting children's self-esteem at great cost to the individual, schools and human growth.

Daniel Goleman (1996) in his best-selling book Emotional Intelligence made huge claims for the importance of emotional intelligence. The cover of the book states that it will tell the reader "Why it can matter more than IQ". This book was to become the foundation for the UK self-esteem revolution. Gardner disagrees with the idea of expanding intelligence to include motivation, character and personality. Surely emotional intelligence is just one part of intelligence itself?

Professor Jerome Kagen warned of the dangers of labelling people 'emotionally intelligent' (Gibbs, 1995). As discussed earlier, labelling people can be dangerous. If we begin to measure people on emotional intelligence and designed an indicator we could find ourselves in a similar position to the stigma as not being clever at school. We need more time, more failure and more development.Research has shown that, in fact, how much emotional intelligence matters to the general population and, in particular, children's development has never been proven (Craig, 2007). Maybe one of the reasons why emotional intelligence has caught on so much is because current work seems to suggest that IQ doesn't matter?

The Self-Esteem *Curriculum*?

After the Second World War and the aptly dubbed 'baby boomers', the self-esteem of children boomed in America in the '80s and '90s. Studies show that the number of psychology and education journal articles, devoted to self-esteem doubled between the 1970s and the 1980s. Journals on self-esteem increased another 52% during the 1990s (Hewitt, 1998). Magazines, TV and many books emphasised the importance of self-esteem for children.There seemed to be an underlying misconception that self-esteem can and should be taught. When self-esteem programs are used, studies show that children are encouraged to believe that it is acceptable and desirable to be preoccupied with and praise oneself (Hewitt, 1998). Most of these programs encourage children to feel good about themselves for no particular reason. In other words, feeling good about yourself is more important than performance. Rita Kramer after spending a year sitting in American teacher training courses in Universities and observing lessons, in '*Ed School Follies, The Miseducation of America's teachers*' found that:

> "*Many teacher-training courses in America became pre-occupied with emphasising that a child's self-esteem must be preserved amongst all else. Perhaps as a result, 60% of teachers and 69% of school counsellors in America agreed that self-esteem should be raised by providing more unconditional validation of students based on who they are, rather than how they behave or perform.*" (P33)

I argue that unconditional validation of students based on who they are, rather than how they behave or perform is highly dangerous to mental health. I argue that self-esteem without any foundation encourages laziness rather than hard work. Psychology research shows, true self-confidence comes from honing your talents and learning things, not from being told you are wonderful just because you exist (Jennifer Crooker *et al*, 2004). Studies show that the practice of not correcting mistakes, avoiding letter grades and discouraging competition is very misguided, for example, competition can be brilliant for children. The recent effort of young people in the Paralympics in London 2012 is just one example of this. (Twenge, 2006 & Stout, 2000). The self–esteem movement is popular because it is so sweetly addictive: teachers don't have to criticise, no one has to fail, hence the pupils' self-esteem remains high and everyone is number one.In the UK, in a DfES (2007) *Department for Education and Skills Primary Guidance* document recommending social and emotional learning; the following quote is taken from the opening paragraph in Appendix 4:

> *"Research on 'emotional intelligence' has brought a wider view of 'Intelligence' to include personal and social issues. Emotional and social competences have been shown to be more influential than cognitive abilities for personal, career and scholastic success, so they need to be central to school and learning to increase school effectiveness. Working in this area can improve educational and life chances."* (P5 – 8)

Yet again, we are fixated on success and let us not forget that how much emotional intelligence matters to the general population and, in particular, children's development has to date never been proven. In studies on depression, it has been shown how an introspection and excessive amount of emotional awareness can lead to paralysing self-centeredness and wading through an unpleasant emotional state rather than trying to deal with the original problem (Weare, 2004).

Weare & Gray (2003) were commissioned by the DfES to write a report called *What Works in Developing Children's Emotional and Social Competence and Wellbeing?* It was published in 2003. The researchers' remit was to undertake a study examining how a child's emotional and social competence and well-being could most effectively be developed at national and local level. In the report the authors, on their own admission, do not undertake a 'systematic review' of the literature. Their findings were disturbing. It was found that we don't know how to talk about emotional intelligence and need a greater understanding of the terms:

> *"Given the range of terminology that is in use in the field, it would be helpful for DfES and the many professionals involved to develop a greater understanding*

and awareness of the range of terms involved, and work towards achieving greater commonality of terminology." (P5)

A need for more evaluation was highlighted and that we do not know enough about emotional intelligence yet:

"There is a need for much more evaluation which uses controls where appropriate and, as a minimum, 'before and after' evaluation. It is recommended that DfES does more both to encourage and finance such evaluation." (P6)

They prioritised it:

"There is strong international evidence to suggest that a whole school approach is vital in effectively promoting emotional and social competence and wellbeing. Many of those working in this field believe that a higher priority should be given to the promotion of emotional and social competence and wellbeing at national, LEA and school level. At the same time, DfES is urged to acknowledge the perceived tensions between any future work in this area, and the feelings of some LEAs and schools that they are already under great pressure and would find it difficult to take forward new initiatives." (P7)

They found that due to the current obsession with success that teachers had so much to deal with that they are feeling very stressed and recommended a promotion of teachers' well-being and competence:

"There is good evidence that teachers cannot transmit emotional and social competence and wellbeing effectively if their own emotional and social needs are not met. At the same time, there are indications that teachers feel very stressed at present." (P7)

Also in this report surfaces the fact that there are no standard measures or indicators for this work. This was the first in depth report of this kind until 2005 where it was found that the construct of emotional intelligence remained debatable and using self-esteem programs may usefully contribute to children's development. Then Colleen McLoughlin (2008) reviewed emotional intelligence programs in schools and found that: it was actually dangerous to solely adopt an individualistic [emotional Intelligence] programmatic approach. She suggested that we need a wider emphasis on teaching, relationships and community building with young people. So, in short, in our ten year journey with emotional intelligence in my opinion, we can conclude that self-esteem programs do not work, the political climate of the teaching profession currently causes stress to the individual teachers and what works best, is what has always works best, learning from our elders and specialists, where we live and positive relationships.

Emotional Intelligence is a valid and a very interesting topic. At an adult and professional level it is useful and powerful. The idea that emotional intelligence should maybe be used in leadership is primarily where its best results have come from. Research shows that to be a successful head teacher, personal qualities, especially in the area of emotional intelligence are necessary (Brighouse, 2006).

I argue that the behaviours of school leaders' have a much greater impact on pupil performance than school structures or leadership models; much of the work by the NCSL (National College for Schools Leadership) supports this. I have no doubt that emotional intelligence will yield advancements in psychology and the study of intelligence, however we must be patient and not rush something so complex through into contact with our children.

Narcissism

> *'The narcissist devours people, consumes their output, and*
> *casts the empty, writhing shells aside.'*
> – Sam Vaknin

Narcissism is a trait that almost all psychologists agree is completely negative. It means: excessive self-importance and in the west, it is on the rise. It encourages perfectionist tendencies and in some cases the proportions of their perfection becomes so ridiculous, they believe that they can never fail and are indeed perfect. Research has shown that we look upon ourselves in general, in a favourable light (Biswas-Diener, 2012). Narcissism, however, is like a perverted and twisted version of this. The sexualisation of children is horrendous. Advertisers have been targeting children and like an infection, sowing the seeds of consumerist ideas. More and more younger children are exposed to sexual images and the message seems to be, you have to be sexy to be accepted.

The media has created such strong stereotypes and metaphors that some people genuinely believe they are much more important than they actually are, they are not losers, they are not stupid and they certainly do not fail… Perfection is the aim and, as we know, perfection is impossible; we are locked into a harmful partnership. Even people who fit the external stereotype of perfect looks will still question themselves. I argue that perfectionism is perfectionism's undoing. Who decided we should be aiming for this? Research has shown that getting what you think you want is consistently overrated as a source of happiness and not getting it is overrated as a source of unhappiness (Haidt, 2006).

Narcissism is an aggressive defence strategy that I believe to be unnecessary and hurtful to others. Over time people set up what I call a *narcissistic self-schema*, a narcissistic set of beliefs that people function on. When their self-worth or self-esteem is threatened, people will dig in and defend, often with aggression or rubbishing other people's opinions, attitudes and putting others down. Research has shown that the core ingredient for narcissism is a fragile and unstable form of self-esteem called *contingent self-esteem* (Kernis and Paradise, 2002). This occurs when people's sense of their own worth is reliant on meeting specific external standards. Tim Kasser (2002) gives an example of this when people feel their self-worth hinges on a grade they receive in a test or compliment. When people with contingent self-esteem are successful with their objectives they do get positive re-affirming feelings but these tend to be short lived and soon the next danger, threat, challenge or failure... will occur.

One can draw parallels with contingent self-esteem and materialistic values. Research by Tim Kasser (2002) has shown that values of money, fame and image cluster together because they focus on extrinsic concerns. Contingent self-esteem, like extrinsic goals are hinged on whether there is some sort of reward. I argue that the key to developing a healthy balance of self-esteem is to evoke positive failure. There is an overwhelming amount of research to show that contingent self-esteem is present in narcissism. (Kasser, 2002, Kanner and Gomes, 1995, Kohut, 1971 & Miller, 1981). Research has shown that narcissists often attempt to cover their feelings of inadequacy by going to the opposite extreme; they hide behind a false sense of worth that is typically dependant on external accomplishments and other people telling them that they are wonderful. We must stop removing challenges, lowering the grade boundaries and telling people they are great just because they are who they are. In fact, if anything people with contingent self-esteem desperately need to learn how to fail.

Narcissism has been on the increase for a long time. Newsom *et al* (2003) found, that in the early 1950s only 12% of teenagers aged 14–16 agreed with the statement 'I am an important person'. By the late 1980s an incredible 80% claimed they were important. Psychologist Harrison Gough (1991) also found consistent increases on narcissism between the 1960s and the 1990s. Studies have shown that many students in the UK and USA at school display entitlement. A notion of the idea that they are 'owed' a particular grade. A feature of narcissism that involves believing that you deserve, and are entitled to more than others. (Irvine, 2005, Stout, 2000 & Twenge, 2006). In a set of laboratory studies Bushman *et al* (2003) found that narcissistic men felt less empathy for rape victims, reported more enjoyment when watching a rape scene in a movie and were more punitive toward a woman who refused to read a sexually arousing passage out loud to them. I believe that a pseudoscientific and paranoid focus by governments on self-esteem is occurring, is breeding narcissism and it has to stop.

Materialism

"The best things in life aren't things."
– Art Buchwald

Materialism has been steadily infecting our families, children and teenagers. Parents sometimes use materialism to *'win over'* children. Children will want 'things' as they are maliciously and unscrupulously targeted by the media and manipulated into wanting things they often don't even understand, let alone need. You cannot 'buy' love. When buying them new clothes and substituting failure in a loving setting for items, serious problems begin to occur. Studies show that if we consistently offer our children products as opposed to relationship experiences and failure, then they are denied the opportunity to learn about people and in particular to recognise and value the needs and feelings of others (Gerhardt, 2010). The focus on materialism since the Second World War has had a drastic impact on education. As materialism is very much extrinsic, by tying oneself to possessions and *'things'* one is showing traits similar to contingent self-esteem.

As technology advances we seem to be working longer and harder, and be connected in some way all the time. Social networking websites and machines have almost become like ghosts of psychological connection. Making us feel that we are connected when we are actually not. To try and avoid the advertising and media onslaught is very difficult and near impossible. I argue that, being isolated seems to be financially rewarding for the consumerist companies as it keeps us buying. Research has shown that despite the technological advances the quality of life is lower and that biologically we trust what we see with our own eyes, so living in a cropped, edited and consumerist world comes with its own psychological dangers (Robinson, 2001 & Brown, 2010) Tim Kasser (2002) draws a definite link between materialism and self-esteem. He found that people who are strongly focused on materialistic values were often raised in non-nurturing environments that poorly satisfied their needs for security and safety. Research has shown that pupils and students in deprived areas are much more materialistic than in affluent areas (Rosenburg, 1965).

Surely though, money does make a difference to how satisfied we are with our lives? Martin Seligman (2011) explains how gross domestic product (GDP) was, during the industrial revolution a decent first approximation to how well a nation was doing. Now, however, every time we build a prison, every time there is a divorce, a motor accident, or a suicide, the GDP goes up. With a large sum of money, we could pay our bills, get a big house, set up our family and friends and buy that boat in the Caribbean? Studies show that people's life satisfaction does not change regardless of an increase in earnings and GDP. Even a study showing comparison between lottery winners to average earning people found that lottery winners became less satisfied with everyday events than the average earners (Brickman *et al*, 1978).

Our students/teenagers live in a highly sophisticated world of coffee houses, high fashion, strong media stereotypes and an obsession with success. I argue that there is a growing perfectionist tendency. In addition to this the academic pressure is changing, research has shown that there has been a huge change in expectations of young people over the past ten years. More and more young people are going into higher education and the entry standards at the top have risen (O'Connor & Sheehy, 2000). This paradigm is exploited by consumerism. Once people have 'it' they habituate and adapt, then want a new 'it', they are locked into a never-ending upgrade. Brickman and Campbell (1971) coined this term as the 'hedonic treadmill'. Like a hamster wheel it will just keep going round and round.

According to the multiple discrepancy theory, our level of satisfaction is determined by the comparisons we make between our current circumstances and multiple standards (Michalos, 1985). So if the people around us are millionaires and we are not, our situation does not seem as favourable as if we are shop assistants surrounded by people in poverty. My instant reaction to this was that millionaires do not surround me. Until I really thought about it, actually they do. We only have to look at the advertising campaigns, magazines, television or Internet. It is corrosive and unrelenting. Studies have shown that when we measure our success against the standards presented in the media rather than the best in our immediate reference group, this can lead to unhappiness because we cannot attain the standards set by media images (Myers, 1992, Wood, 1996 & Buss, 2000). This is congruent with Zahavi and Zahavi (1997) who also cite the ability to compare oneself to others as an 'obstacle to happiness'. This idea of comparing oneself to others is an important point in the distinction between ones perception of success or failure. One may have succeeded compared to some but failed according to others.

It is important that children are made aware of the colossal power and influence that the media has on them. This can be achieved by making parents aware, explaining adverts and open discussion. Frome and Eccles (1998) suggested a sceptical approach to the media. Eccles found that parents' tendency to purvey stereotyped theories to their children reflected uncritical exposure to those ideas in television shows and magazines. We have to teach our children to criticise, think for themselves and how to have the courage to fail.

Self-Deception and Self-Justification

"Reality denied comes back to haunt."
– Philip K. Dick

We can have interesting reactions to failure when, unavoidably, we come into unprepared frontal and full-contact with it. It is important to gain an understanding of the defences we employ, that in many instances are now redundant, de-habilitating and holding us back. I argue that we all *subconsciously* want to be right, all the time. Hypothetically, let's imagine a world where this happens. Every endeavour succeeds as well as you thought it would, every obstacle is overcome easily and any problem is immediately solved. To me, this feels uncomfortable and frightening. Something ironically wouldn't be *'right'* if this was reality. Many of us overcome huge challenges and difficulties before we even leave the womb. We subconsciously strive to keep our image of ourselves positive yet we all know that everyone makes mistakes and nobody's perfect. So why do we defend, pretend and, in some cases, twist the truth to make ourselves look good?

For many years it has been thought that competition ensures the best outcome. When we are in competition, by the very definition of the word, we are protective. This is a direct extension of the failure heterodoxy; we hold our best ideas close and become very attached to them. What if they fail? Where do we turn?

What would happen if we embraced our own vulnerability rather than shunned it. We all know that we are not perfect? So why do we act as if this is the case? Research has shown that openness and connectivity may in the end be far more valuable to innovation than purely competitive mechanisms. Throughout history, civilisations have built walls around their cities, their towns and their ideas, and throughout history time after time, the walls have crumbled, fractured physically and mentally and they have or will eventually fail. Writing was once restricted from the common people by monks, as it was thought it would cause mass anarchy. The exception to this is nature that has very few boundaries. From bees pollinating flowers to the remarkable mutually beneficial relationships across species, the achievements and successes of nature far outweigh our own. I believe that this is because nature is prepared to fail. Research by Steven Johnson (2010) explains how environments that block or limit those new combinations by punishing experimentation, obscuring certain branches of possibility, making the current state so comfortable that no one bothers to explore the edge, will generally generate fewer innovations than environments that encourage exploration.

We seem to find it hugely important to maintain a positive view of ourselves, and the world around us, we use a subconscious and conscious battery of defences and self–deceptive strategies to manage negative information. These may hold the key to explaining why failure is avoided in such copious quantities. Research shows that self-deceptive strategies are not all bad; they bring us peace and enable relaxation. They ease the sting of embarrassment. However, without an awareness of this and without reasonable grounds self-justification, without evidence or reality can hide our errors and failures sabotaging our ability to learn (Tavris and Aronson, 2008).

I believe that self-justification and cognitive dissonance provide the reason why failure has remained heterodoxy for so long. After a person has failed, it can be tempting to compare yourself to someone less competent. Research has shown that people will go to extraordinary and humiliating lengths to restore their sense of worth after a failure. (Tesser, 2000, Gollwitzer & Wicklund, 1985).

If one believes in fixed intelligence, then defences are necessary for when you make a mistake or fail. This will undoubtedly slow, or indeed stop learning. Studies have shown that when intelligence is seen as fixed, nothing can be done to truly enhance it and people turn to defensive strategies. People seem to expose themselves to information or even perverted information to make themselves feel good again. (Elliot and Dweck, 2005). If we accept this framework, it is a waste of time to artificially prop yourself up when you could be re-dedicating yourself to the failure itself. Sociologically speaking, we are nothing special. A multitude of research has shown that our own talents and attributes are broadly normal and not exceptional and that we have limited control over an unpredictable, chaotic world and our own impulses. (Taylor, 1989 & Taylor and Brown,1988 & 1994). This is in direct contrast to what is often portrayed in the western media.

Most people, when directly confronted with evidence that they are wrong, will not change their point of view or course of action, but will dig in and justify it even more. If we are not prepared to admit we have failed, then how can we learn from it? We seem to often be able to admit failure, however avoid responsibility and accountability. Tavris and Aronson (2008) explain how between the conscious lie to fool others and the unconscious self-justification, lurks much confusion. Our memory is fallible and, I argue, that our own ego enhancing tendency as human beings can get in the way of learning; if you lie to yourself for long enough, you will believe yourself.

A common defence used is described by Melanie Klein in Burton (2010) who describes how we also use 'manic defence' when presented with uncomfortable feelings or thoughts. We distract the conscious mind either with a flurry of activity or with opposite thoughts or feelings. We can gain a further understanding of this bizarre facet of human psychology by looking at how we react to traumas. For some, failing at school is a trauma that they do not recover from. According to Joseph and Linley's (2005) model of *Organismic Valuing Theory of Growth through Adversity*, much of post-traumatic growth or stress seems to stem from whether the person has either a rigid set of beliefs or has the ability to change their viewpoint and adapt. It can be necessary to create positive illusions. Research has shown that most people are biased to viewing themselves in an optimistic light, have an unrealistic sense of personal control and have an unfounded sense of optimism that the future will be better than the facts suggest (Csikzentmihayli,1992, Taylor, 1989, Biswas-Diener, 2012). Taylor (1989) concluded that most people, especially healthy people, are biased towards viewing themselves in an optimistic way. She argues that defences like denial and repression distort reality. The brain that 'knows' the dirty secret becomes disconnected.

Over 50 years ago, Leon Festinger (1957) named the key driver behind self-justification as the unpleasant feeling; cognitive dissonance. Tavris and Aronson (2008) describe cognitive dissonance as a state of tension whenever a person holds two cognitions *(ideas, beliefs, opinions)* that are psychologically inconsistent. Such as: *'I am a clever student but I failed.'* Dissonance produces an uncomfortable mental feeling. The most direct way to reduce the dissonance would be for the student to work harder or retake the test. Often, due to the contributing factors of labelling students, pressure on teachers and pupils, the various schemes and strategies of groundlessly raising self-esteem and the failure heterodoxy, this does not happen. What often happens is the student finds a way to reduce the dissonance in such ways as saying; *'I am not bothered'.*

Festinger and Aronson (1957) began testing and working on the dissonance theory. This theory directly challenged many notions that were set in stone in psychology at the time. Their research predicted that if people go through a great deal of pain, discomfort, effort or embarrassment to get something, they will be happier and more satisfied with that something than if it came to them easily. This experiment was repeated many times with the clear outcome that if a person voluntarily goes through a difficult or a painful experience in order to attain some goal or object, that goal or object becomes more attractive. Research on dissonance theory also made obsolete the idea that we as humans process information logically. If the new information we find is consistent with our beliefs, we think it is well founded and useful: *'just what I always said.'*

However, if the new information doesn't fall in line with our beliefs, then we consider it biased or silly, this mental contortion the *conformation bias* (Nickerson, 1998) is congruent with Buss's (2000) ideas about the pseudoscientific beliefs that raising self-esteem without grounds will improve achievement, which is currently used in UK Education policy. Neuroscientists, Western and Kilts *et al* (2006) have recently shown that these biases in thinking are built into the way our brain processes information. In a study of people who were being monitored by magnetic resonance imaging (MRI) whilst they were trying to process dissonant or consonant information when shown groundless evidence that their false belief was true they observed a calming effect with the consonant information as opposed to the truth which created a more agitated state.

Rhodewalt (1994) introduces the idea of self–handicapping strategies, for example, not studying until the last minute before an exam. This makes any subsequent failure less reflective of ability. Although this increases the stakes and makes failure far more likely, it has a get out clause. One is then in a good position to blame the failure on the self-handicapping strategy. His research also showed that that students who believed that ability was fixed, were more likely to engage in self-handicapping than students who believed the incremental theory of intelligence and pursued learning goals. The fixed view fosters strategies that are negative for learning and orientated more to self-esteem protection, whereas the malleable view fosters strategies that are conducive to the growth of real competence and skill. Biswas-Diener (2012) explains how self-handicapping is not the healthiest psychological approach to failure, and it undermines the moral element of courage.

Extensive research by Taylor and Brown (1989),(1988) and (1994) has shown that positive illusions involve the cognitive processes of selective attention, benign forgetting, maintaining pockets of incompetence, and maintaining negative self-schemas. Research has shown how negative information about the self can also be managed by creating an area of incompetence and accepting it. By not using information about our performance in these domains, in evaluating our self-worth, self-esteem is preserved (Carr, 2004).

This is partly the problem with the work of *strengths* in positive psychology. By focusing just on what we are good at and chasing performance in learning, we can easily neglect our weaknesses and stop investing effort in them. An example may be – *I didn't do well in my exam because I am shy and my shyness prevented me from asking questions in the class.*

Research shows that the belief in control reduces stress responses (Carr and Wilde, 1988). As an example, in games of chance, Langer (1975) found that if there is any information that suggests that winning is due to skill, like introducing a well-dressed expert at a game who shows how it is done, people behave as if rolling a dice or picking a card is a skilled activity. Most of us do create positive illusions, so as teachers' research shows that the best way to correct pupils' failures, quickly and accurately. Psychologically speaking, Carr (2004) suggests that the best way to modify these is if the subject is given negative information in a way that is corrective but not devastating. It is important that this is not taken too far, as trauma, victimisation and loss can shatter positive illusions and prevent people from seeing the self as good. That is where long lasting damage can be done.

What about when we can't even see our failures? Kathryn Schulz (2010) in her work on being wrong found that if our current mistakes or failures are unseen, even when we really look deep inside ourselves, then it makes complete logical sense for us to arrive at the conclusion that we are correct. She draws a parallel with the unseen mistakes and error as a reason why we do accept that nobody is perfect and we all get it wrong, yet we are continually surprised by our own failures, errors and mistakes.

SCHOOL EXAM QUESTION:
5. Who said, 'I think therefore I am'?
Answer: I did.

Positive Failure

Chapter **Three**
Failure: Some Insights from Positive Psychology

Most of the shadows of this life are caused by standing in one's own sunshine.
– Ralph Waldo Emerson

Positive failure has its roots in positive psychology. To begin with let us look at this emerging field and our inherent negativity bias. Positive psychology is a new branch of psychology and positive failure is a new branch of positive psychology. What happens when you ask the question: What is right? What is working? And how can we do more of it?

The following are some insights from the field of positive psychology. This chapter offers many illuminating facets and areas of study that help to dispel the poor reputation failure has. I believe the following topics are useful, engaging and the most relevant to failure. I do not attend that this is a complete introduction to the subject.

It is widely regarded that Martin Seligman is the father of the movement; however, it can be traced back to Aristotle. It wasn't until Seligman started asking new questions that it really took off. He began on August 21st 1999 at his presidential address to the annual convention of the American Psychological Association in Boston, USA. He said, *'Psychology is good, but not good enough.'*

Psychology had been primarily focused on fixing what is wrong. The very language of psychology has negative connotations, and through the media, words such as psycho, mental, shrink and the phrase *'sick in the head'* all ring slight alarm bells. Much of the research in psychology is around disorders, trauma, schizophrenia, depression and anxiety. Therapists usually ask what's wrong and consultants in an organisation brought in to fix a problem often first ask what is wrong. We remember horrendous plane crashes, tsunamis and earthquakes much more vividly than the thousands of car accidents that take place, even though we are at much more risk of them. People who are afraid of flying are much more commonly found than people who are afraid of driving. Linely (2008) details how we all, to some degree, focus on the negative, on what's wrong, on what isn't working. We have a negativity bias, bad is stronger than good. Roy Baumeister *et al* (2001) proved it. Sad but true.

Someone who is sad around us is more likely to make us feel sad than the reverse. Our negativity bias has enabled us to survive. When the sabre-toothed tiger appeared at the mouth of our cave, it was this bias that led us to fight it, as opposed to giving it a hug because it was furry. I argue that attending to the negative is adaptive. Now things are different. In most western cities and towns we have clean running water, hospitals, doctors and are in nowhere as much danger as we were. I believe that because we have been so focused on surviving for so long, we have neglected the positive.

I argue that success can breed contempt, whilst positive failure breeds progression. There is a strong antidote to the negativity bias: positive events, emotions and experiences. Barbara Frederickson and Marcial losoda (2005) found a ratio of 3:1, three positive events, emotions or experiences in balance to every negative one. There is a limit, when the positives reached over 11, people got stuck going round in circles. Positive psychology sets out to look at what works, how we can do it better, and includes such topics as strengths, self-efficacy, motivation, emotional intelligence, love, optimism and hope, amongst others. It is a growing branch of psychology and includes a new way of looking at learning that has much to offer education around the world. In the self-determination theory (SDT) Ryan & Deci (2000) describes the basic three psychological needs for humans, as being strong positive senses of autonomy, relatedness and competence. This can be seen by, thinking of a time when you were at your happiest. Then apply the theory above. Whatever or whenever it was you probably had a lot of choice or involvement in the choice of experience or task *(high autonomy)*; it probably involved one or more close relationships *(high relatedness)* and you probably felt competent *(high competence)*. In contrast if you think of a time when you were deeply unhappy, the above needs will not be met. They will all be low, for example, no choice, few or no relationships with other people and a feeling of incompetence.

The following are a set of insights that are helpful as we examine failure and may provide the basis for an answer to the failure heterodoxy.

Strength and Courage

A hero is an ordinary individual who finds the strength to persevere
and endure in spite of overwhelming obstacles.
– Christopher Reeve

What are your strengths? What are you really good at? I argue that we don't really have the language to define strengths and often find talking about them uneasy and threatening, for fear of being seen as arrogant. Recently in the field of positive psychology, much work has been conducted around strengths. The basic idea is, each person has different strengths and your best performance will come from honing these rather than focusing on your weaknesses.

Alex Linely (2008), the founding member of CAPP (Centre for Applied Positive

Psychology) in his book, *"Average to A*: Realising Strengths in Yourself and Others"* defines a strength as follows:

> *"Strength is a pre-existing capacity for a particular way of behaving, thinking or feeling that is authentic and energising to the user, and enables optimal functioning, development and performance." (P9)*

In the book he also identifies five fundamentals of the strengths approach as he sees them. They are:

> *"(1) The strengths approach focuses on what is right, what is working and what is strong.*
> *(2) Strengths are part of our basic human nature; therefore every person in the world has strengths and deserves respect for their strengths.*
> *(3) Our areas of greatest potential are in the areas of our greatest strength.*
> *(4) We succeed by fixing our weaknesses only when we are making the best of our strengths.*
> *(5) Using our strengths is the smallest thing we can do to make the biggest difference."(P5)*

So as you grow up and go through life, he believes that although these elements may change, your core personality and basic strengths will remain the same. The fact that strengths enable *optimal functioning and development* refers to the idea that using your strengths allows you to be at your best in terms of psychological functioning. Studies have shown that particular strengths are relevant to particular environments. This is called the law of parsimony (Linely, 2008). We should be able to do the greatest number of things, tasks etc, with the smallest possible number of strengths. Interpersonal skills for relating to a rival warrior trying to plunder our land are not a strength we need anymore. However interpersonal skills in general are. This begs the question: are there universal strengths that all human beings have? Peterson and Seligman (2004) developed a classification of character strengths and virtues from 117,676 participants drawn from 54 different nations from around the world. They believed they found universally valued and identifiable strengths across different cultures and different historical periods. There are 24, grouped into 6 areas:

- Strengths of Wisdom and Knowledge: Creativity, Curiosity, Open-mindedness, Love of Learning and Perspective
- Strengths of Courage: Bravery, Persistence, Integrity, Vitality
- Strengths of Humanity: Love, kindness, Social Intelligence
- Strengths of Justice: Citizenship, Fairness, Leadership

- Strengths of Temperance: Forgiveness, Humility, Prudence, Self-regulation
- Strengths of Transcendence: Appreciation of Beauty, Gratitude, Hope, Humour and Spirituality

These categories were used as the basis of the VIA (values in action) Strengths assessment which have been taken by nearly 2 million people.Sometimes we can have strengths that we don't even realise are our strengths. These *unrealised strengths* are often identified by things/tasks/achievements that come easily to us. We can sometimes think that everyone has the same skills and talents as us, particularly teenagers and what we do is nothing special, because everyone else can do it, too. Unrecognised strengths can be found often by becoming frustrated with others as they find the same task much more challenging than you.

Do you ever hold back, disengage or not take part because you do not want to look arrogant? Alex Linley (2008) believes that the strengths approach should be about being the best we can be not trying to be better than anyone else. I believe that schools often teach to compete rather than co-operate and, if a highly competitive culture is embedded in a school *(which does have benefits)* one of the things can happen is that children can feel pressurised into not using their strengths for fear of the social and emotional embarrassment.

I believe and have found that when using strengths, we often do not accept positive feedback for fear of a ramification or for a fear of future failures. Research by Linely (2008) has found five embedded reasons why we seem to be unable to accept positive feedback:

"We are concerned about being seen as arrogant; We fear becoming complacent; We risk pressure and the threat of mistakes from even higher expectations of us; As we raise the expectation we increase the risk of failure; We do not see the positive ourselves."(P114 – 115)

I argue that often positive feedback is seen as part of the commonly termed feedback sandwich; *(something you're doing wrong, something you're doing right, then something you've done wrong)* this can be seen as made up, false and frustrates people. Linely (2008) suggests a framework for positive feedback. One should make sure that it is:

"Specific: it is tied to a particular event or moment in time
Targeted: because it is about a particular behaviour or action
With evidence: because of the outcome to which it led is encompassed as a core part of the positive feedback message."(P117)

Some studies have shown that strength is a combination of: talent, knowledge and skills (Clifton and Harter, 2003). I define this further as a talent being: *naturally recurring patterns of thought feeling or behaviour, or something that you do, however do not understand why others find it hard*. Knowledge being the elements you can change or invest time in often at school. Finally, the skill is the sum of these two parts together, sometimes a grade and sometimes not. A metaphor can be drawn to a lump of coal containing the diamond. It is very often the knowledge and investment of effort and time that creates the diamond *(skill)*. I, in Lewis (2011) argue that talent itself, whilst it can't be ignored, deserves little merit. Very little effort is invested in a talent. It is very often the knowledge and investment of effort and time that creates the skill.

We often look at children's school reports and if they have a good grade in that subject, teachers can assume that that is where their strength is. Without knowledge of strengths, we all too often push children into what Linley (2008) describes as *learned behaviours*. Just because a child got an A* in Maths doesn't mean that they want to be a mathematics professor. For the child it is difficult because achieving feels good, if they are pushed into something without thought they will often be promoted quickly and will search for satisfaction in the money, reward or respect rather than the Maths itself. I suggest that there are only so many promotions, rewards and merits before people suffer diminished interest, effort, motivation and finally competence.

Strengths are a noble idea and there is much evidence to support them. There is a danger, however, by focusing on strengths (which is usually what we enjoy and find relatively easy) we can ignore our weaknesses. There are downsides of strengths, one of which is the fact that VIA Strengths test does not account for weaknesses. It also places the same value on the strength; 'appreciation of beauty' as the 'strength of bravery.' Also, by focusing on our strengths to the exclusion of our weaknesses are we being naïve? Linely (2008) believes that we should make weaknesses irrelevant. I agree. There are things you can do when you know and accept your weaknesses, such as delegating or working with other people with contrasting strengths. Research suggests that you can even listen for strengths in people (Linley, 2008).

Strengths are worthwhile and an advancement, however, looking more closely, we have only begun to scratch the surface.

SCHOOL EXAM QUESTION:
6. Upon ascending the throne the first thing Queen Elizabeth II did was to..?
Answer: Sit down.

Virtues

What do we mean by virtues? Or being virtuous? Robbins and Friedman (2011) describe how throughout the long tradition of virtue theory, virtues have been understood as *arête* or *excellence*. Fowers (2005) describes virtues as the character strengths that enable individuals to pursue their own goals, ideals and to excel as human beings. The virtuous person is not one who on the off chance acts in a good ethical way but intentionally sets their own moral compass to good. Ethics are linked to the subject of virtues. If one uses a virtue towards a bad/evil end then it becomes a vice. Fowers (2005) goes on to argue that the positive psychology approach to virtue, treats virtues as isolated variables that are logically dependant on each other. I argue that this is not the case and that logic has very little to do with it. I agree with Aristotle's philosophy, which is described by Schwartz and Sharpe (2005); for Aristotle the virtues were understood to be interdependent, reliant on each other and therefore, he thought must be approached holistically and with a sense of hierarchy, which is the humanistic psychology stance. I argue that virtues need to be understood as relating to the whole person, not traits by themselves that we own. Master virtues are networks that grow. Continuing with the idea that all virtues are interconnected, I argue they are also not equal. Schwartz and Sharpe (2005) explain how some virtues operate as master (superordinate) virtues. Master virtues regulate subordinate virtues so they do not become subverted into becoming vice when put into practice.

The construct of hardiness is a good construct to illustrate how one might conceptualise resilience as a superordinate or master virtue. One of the most common virtues that I hear parents talk about and yearn for is their children to be resilient upon leaving school. Perhaps this is the failure 'immunity' that perhaps we should be striving for? According to Maddi (2006) in *'The Courage to Grow from Stresses'* hardiness is conceptualised as composed of three attitudes: commitment, control and challenge.

> *"Commitment: This consists of the decision to remain engaged with people and events in one's life even when faced with great stress*
> *Control: This is the effort to continue to affect the events in one's life, rather than falling into a passive mode of engagement*
> *Challenge: The tendency for people to consider adversity as an opportunity for cultivating wisdom." (P160-168)*

I argue that hardiness and resiliency as superordinate virtues would likely both be a combination of subordinate virtues. I argue that positive failure is the fuel, the spark to set off this chain reaction which is needed for both the master virtues of resilience and practical wisdom. I argue, as do Robbins and Friedman (2011) that many truly outstanding individuals, and the most resilient among us, are able to withstand temporary displeasure and misery for the sake of a greater, future good. It is argued by Sartor (2003), Thurman (2005) and Wegela (2009) that some degree of suffering in life is necessary for the cultivation of wisdom. Miller (2003) commented on how resiliency may also include post-traumatic growth, in which the person's quality of life is actually improved after having survived adverse circumstances.

Positive and negative failures in themselves are not ethical concepts in any form. In fact if anything they can bring negative feelings. They create hardiness, as conceptualised by Maddi (2006). However, as they lead to the master virtues (or vices) of resilience and in turn *Phronesis*, ethics does enter into the equation. Aristotle understood the goodness of any virtue to be inseparable from the goodness of the ends of the virtue. If a virtuous trait were to lead to evil, it would therefore not be a virtue at all but a vice – a virtue perverted into a disposition towards evil, rather than goodness. Therefore in the case of resiliency, the resilient aspects of a person should not be considered a virtue unless and until, that personal strength is used for benevolent ends. The question of what is benevolent and what is malevolent is a difficult one, and is subjective. In short, we are very keen (in good old fashioned human fashion) to try and find a shortcut to building resilience without failure. I go as far as to argue that it is near impossible to amass true resilience without failure.

A great example of this is shown in Seligman (2011), by a leading General of the US Army. The US army now trains all of its soldiers in resilience training. Seligman was willingly recruited to advice on this from a standpoint of developing a Psychological fitness. Seligman (2011) argues that resilience, at least among young civilians, can be taught. This was the main thrust of positive education. He found that depression, anxiety, and conduct problems could be reduced among children and adolescents through resilience training. I argue: for how long? We haven't tested what happens when they leave school and hit the real workforce extensively. I argue that resilience cannot be taught. It has to be cultivated and has a subjective level, which differs in every individual. On a more disturbing note, in Martin Seligman's *'Flourish'*, Richard Carmona, the surgeon general of the US Army under President George Bush, commented:

> *"If we want health, we should concentrate on building resilience - psychologically and physically – particularly among young people. We want a fighting force that can bounce back and cope with persistent warfare that this next decade promises."(P128)*

Are we in danger of endorsing a master vice of resilience, in danger of creating the soldier who feels nothing when children are blown apart as casualties of war?

The Master Virtue of Resilience

I argue that positive failure is conducive to operating in the master virtue of resilience and practical wisdom or 'phronesis'. Kathryn Schulz (2010) in her book: *'Adventures in the Margin of Error'* offers this description or error and the ideas that shape it:

> "In ancient Indo- European, the ancestral language of nearly half of today's global population, the word er meant 'to move', 'to set in motion' or simply 'to go'. That root gave rise to the Latin verb errare, meaning to wander or, more rakishly, 'to roam'. The Latin in turn gave us the English word 'erratic' used to describe movement that is unpredictable or aimless. And of course it gave us 'error'. From the beginning then, the idea of error has contained a sense of motion. Of wandering, seeking, going astray. Implicitly, what we are seeking – and what we have strayed from is the truth.
>
> In the two archetypal wanderers of Western culture we see clearly the contrasting ideas that shape our understanding of error. One of these is the knight errant and the other is the Juif errant – the wandering Jew. The latter figure, a staple of anti-Semitic propaganda, derives from a medieval Christian legend, in which a Jew encountering Jesus on the road to crucifixion taunts him for moving so slowly under the weight of the cross. In response, Jesus condemns the man to roam the earth until the end of time.
>
> As the historian, David Bates has observed: the wandering Jew, literally embodied, for Christian Europeans, the individual separated from the truth. In this model, erring is inextricably linked to both sin and exile. To err is to experience estrangement from God and alienation among men. The knight errant is also a staple of medieval legend, but otherwise he could scarcely be more different. Where the wandering Jew is defined by his sin, the knight errant [operates in the the master virtue of resilience] is distinguished by his virtue; he is explicitly and unfailingly on the side for good. His most famous representatives include Galahad, Lancelot and Gawain, those most burnished of knights in shining armour.
>
> Although far from home, the knight is hardly in exile, and still less in disgrace. Unlike the juif errant who is commanded to wander and does so aimlessly and in misery. The knight errant is on a quest: he wanders on purpose and with purpose as well as with pleasure. He is driven, like all travelers, by curiosity, by the desire to experience something more of the world." (P41-42)

I argue that the model of the 'Juif errant' is so deeply and subconsciously woven sociologically into western culture that this could have been one of the key factors in the growth of the *failure heterodoxy*. Psychologically, there have been many different definitions and ideas of what resilience is. From it being described as a resourceful adaptation to changing circumstances, to the ability to adapt and overcome adversity. Through repeated exposure to positive failure, I argue, one can begin to develop a 'failure immunity' similar to the master virtue of resilience and it will build resilience.

Ideas

For many years we as human kind have lusted after the *good idea*. We have described it often as a stroke of genius, eureka moment and have often attributed it to one person in one moment. New research by Steven Johnson (2010) has shown that ideas are actually not something that happens in isolation or in an illuminating moment. He argues that an idea is a network. A new idea is a new network of neurons firing in sync that has never formed before. I argue that we live in a world where intellectual property is just that, owned property. There are obvious and important reasons for this, and there is weight to the argument against cheating and stealing someone else's ideas. However, it does depend on what the particular goal is and if the goal is progression and learning then to truly learn and progress sharing ideas seems sensible?

Congruent with having a fixed mindset, if we take a protective standpoint on ideas in learning then defences are necessary to protect our property. However when we shift the focus and change our goal from: 'this is my idea', to 'how can we formulate the best idea?' We remove the competition. As Steven exclaims, we connect as opposed to protect our ideas. In my experience many of the best ideas seem to come not from the front line but in the staffrooms, lunch, relaxed sharing of mistakes and ideas and ideas lay in the murky depths sometimes for years before coming to fruition.

Steven Johnson's research (2010) included a study by Kevin Dunbar, who videotaped a laboratory of scientists over a period of time. He observed them at the microscope, at the water cooler, at lunch and he concluded that all the major ideas and breakthroughs happened when people shared their mistakes. I argue that if you are in a supportive environment and connect ideas using positive failure, even laughing at your mistakes, then your ideas will form something so much more valuable than if one is in an unsupportive, isolated and guarded environment. I argue that once we let go of owning an idea, a trait or property, in the same way as the growth mindset operates, we can achieve a higher level of understanding, attainment and progress. The master virtue of resilience is a network and it is interconnected. If we can use the inevitable failure in our own learning and reframe it as positive, build those networks and supportive networks around us, then we will progress the most. It seems that through the sharing of mistakes and the cultivation of practical wisdom that the most progression is made.

SCHOOL EXAM QUESTION:
7. What did Mahatma Ghandi and Genghis Khan have in common?
Answer: Unusual names.

The Growth Mindset

As we explored earlier, calling a child 'low ability' is not acceptable. Furthermore,

Kumar and Jagacinski (2006) found that the belief that ability is fixed undermines people's confidence, even if they keep succeeding. One of the major breakthroughs in psychology is the theory of neuroplasticity, which explores how the brain can change and intelligence is not fixed. LeDoux (1999) has shown that emotion is fundamental to the way the brain functions.

Research by Carol Dweck (2010) identifies two sets of beliefs that people can have about students' intelligence *(and that students can have about their own intelligence)*. They may have a fixed mindset, in which they believe that intelligence is fixed, they are either clever or stupid and this will not change. Or they may have a growth mindset, in which they believe that intelligence can be grown and developed in different ways, effort, instruction and, in my opinion, failure. A growth mindset doesn't imply that everyone is the same, but it does imply that everyone's intellectual ability can grow. Even Einstein wasn't Einstein before he put in years of passionate, relentless effort.

Dweck's work on mindsets is a big deal when it comes to achievement. A massive amount of research has shown that students' mindsets have a direct impact on their grades and, in particular, students who are labouring under a negative stereotype about their abilities. (Blackwell, Trzesniewski & Dweck, 2007, Good, Aronson & Inzlicht, 2003, Blackwell *et al*, 2007, Good *et al*, 2003 & Aronson, Fried & Good, 2002). In teaching how to think with a growth mindset one learns how their brain was like a muscle: the more you use it, the stronger it becomes. Also that every time you stretch yourself to learn something new, your brain forms new connections, and with time you can actually become cleverer.

Working with many pupils over the years, once children realise that they are in control of the growth of their minds, their whole life changes, their attitudes, their positivity, their grades and their confidence. The key to this is that you have to be prepared to fail. Dweck describes how other researchers, Aronson *et al* (2002) and Good *et al* (2003) were finding that teaching a growth mindset raised achievement test scores, however, more importantly as well as students' investment in, and enjoyment of, school. Once students begin to enjoy school then they will try harder, be more resilient and take more risks. I argue that when teachers have a fixed mindset, the students who enter their class as low achievers leave as low achievers at the end of the year. When teachers have a growth mindset though, many of the students who start as low achievers then progress faster and to higher levels. Teachers with a growth mindset are committed to finding routes to make this happen, whatever that may be.

In several studies on the effects of praising students' intelligence as opposed to praising their effort, it was found that when adults praise students' intelligence after a student performs well, they send a fixed mindset message similar to 'you're really clever and that is what has impressed me'.

When adults praise effort or strategies however, they send a growth mindset message saying: 'You have invested a huge amount of effort and tried hard.' (Mueller & Dweck, 1998). I hypothesise that children who are praised for intelligence and then fail are at risk of losing their confidence and motivation, their performance plummeting, and being ashamed of their difficulty. Those whoever, who fail that have been praised for effort, remain resolute and their performance continues to improve. In addition it seems many of them develop a positive yearning for high challenge.

Research has shown that teaching a growth mindset seems to decrease, or even close, achievement gaps (Dweck, 2010). Studies have also shown that when black and Latino students adopt a growth mindset, their grades and achievement test scores look more similar to those of their non-stereotyped peers. This effect is mirrored in different groups, for example, when female students adopt a growth mindset, their grades and achievement test scores in mathematics become similar to those of their male classmates. In these studies, every group seemed to benefit from holding a growth mindset and the stereotyped groups gained the most (Aronson *et al*, 2002, Blackwell *et al*, 2007, Good *et al*, 2003 & Dweck, 2010).

I believe that teachers and administrators need permission to fail and we should all feel free to apply the growth mindset approach. I have found that often in schools the high achievers according to grades have a shockingly low resilience and, should failure rear its head, the emotional and anxiety ridden fallout can cause psychological problems later on. Carol Dweck also discussed the *Imposter syndrome*. This is the belief that your success or achievement is somehow fraudulent, and you are at constant risk of being found out as less bright than you have tricked them to believe you are. One of the many costs of this misconception is having to invest a huge amount of time and effort in trying to prove yourself. This can be very difficult to spot as an educator and can be hidden for years by data, good grades and pressure on schools to produce results.

Covington (1992) defined the motive for self-worth as the desire to establish and maintain a positive self-image, or sense of self-worth. Because children spend so much time in classrooms and are evaluated so frequently there (beginning at 6 or even earlier), Covington argued that protecting ones sense of academic competence Is likely to be critical for maintaining a positive sense of self-worth. Covington and Omelich (1979), describe how, although trying is important for success and is encouraged by teachers and parents, if the children try and fail, then it is difficult to escape the conclusion that they lack ability. Avoiding challenging tasks is a good way to avoid, or minimalise failure experiences. This technique is sadly used by many high achieving students across the country and I would think the world. Carol Dweck's work on growth mindsets was evident in forming part of the *positive failure* theory.

> **Positive failure:** *is failure after appropriate investment that leads to further learning or development.*
> **Negative failure:** *is failure after inappropriate investment that stunts further progress or development. Appropriate investment is just that, and as Dweck states, by improving, cultivating and praising effort rather than ability.*

Optimism and Hope

Optimism and hope seem to be two of the key drivers in positive failure. However, it is important to define optimism properly. If we are optimistic, are we just looking on the bright side and ignoring reality? If we are hopeful, are we deceiving ourselves that life will be better than it actually is? In fact, optimism and hope play a much larger role in failure, learning and competence than one would assume. Without them, it seems we fall ill more frequently, give up quicker and over time become less resilient.

What does it mean to be hopeful? Hope was conceptualised by Professor Rick Snyder as (2000) the ability to plan strategies to desired goals despite obstacles and then employ the motivation to use these strategies. He argues that hope is strongest when it entails valued goals that there is an intermediate probability of attaining, due to challenging but not impossible obstacles. Where we are certain that we will achieve our goals, hope is unnecessary. Where we are certain we will not then we become hopeless. He suggests that hope develops in a clear way through pre-school, childhood and adolescence.

Up until the late 1970s optimism was seen in a negative light; viewed as a sign of immaturity or weakness. A major breakthrough was Matlin and Stang's (1978) work on the *Pollyanna principle* that showed that people's thinking processes were optimistic and most people recalled positive things faster than negative things. Tiger (1979) argued that the capacity to think in an optimistic way was a naturally selected characteristic of our species. Looking on the bright side does seem to have its advantages.

Christopher Peterson (2000) believes that there are two main approaches to optimism. The first, *dispositional optimism*, is defined by Scheier and Carver (1985) as a global expectation that more good than bad will happen in the future. The second, the *Optimistic explanatory style* was conceptualised by Seligman *et al* (1998). He believed that optimism, rather than being a broad personality trait was a way that optimistic people explain negative events or experiences by attributing the cause of these to external, specific factors such as certain situations.

Pessimists, on the other hand, tended to explain negative events or experiences with a more internal approach such as being a personal failure. So, optimists are more likely to say that they failed the exam because the wrong question came up. Pessimists on the other hand are likely to explain the failure because they are not good at academic work.

Optimism is naturally linked to the future time perspective, which I argue, is appropriate to working with children. Research has shown that optimists are different from pessimists in the happiness they enjoy when experiencing adversity. They found that optimists seem to accept the reality of the challenge quicker than pessimists (Scheier, Carver and Bridges, 2001). Seligman (1998) and Gillham (2000) found that in adulthood optimism is associated with better academic achievement, sport performance, occupational adjustment and family life. Not only this, but Peterson and Barret (1987) found that optimism predicts better performance at college and predicts it more accurately than ability measures such as the Scholastic Aptitude test.

Seligmann (1998) has developed programs to help adults and children change their explanatory style from pessimism to optimism. The programs are based on the cognitive therapy models developed by Dr Beck (1976), and Ellis and Harper (1975). Jaycox, Seligman, Reivich & Gillham (1994) in a study entitled *Prevention of depressive symptoms in school children*, claim that the Penn optimism program was designed to help school age children develop optimistic rather than pessimistic explanatory attributional styles and prevent depression. I would simply argue that the biggest impact we can have as teachers is to set up as many situations as possible for our pupils to fail in non-catastrophic ways over time and build their confidence and self-esteem through positive failure as opposed to programs and courses.

Research has found evidence that optimistic people are healthier and happier. Their immune system works better. They cope better with stress and use more effective coping strategies and problem solving (Peterson *et al*, 2000). The process of failing, coming across resistance and overcoming this, I argue, is vital to the creation of hope. Professor Sir Michael Rutter (1994) has likened overcoming such barriers and adversaries to a psychological immunisation process and referred to the outcome as resilience. This conceptualises what positive failure is, almost like a psychological vaccination process for the future or *failure immunisation*. Snyder

(2000) believes that adults with significant hope have experienced just as many failures and setbacks as others in their lives, however, have personified the belief that they are adaptive and can cope with future challenges. They focus on success rather than failure. They experience fewer and less intense negative emotions when they fail or encounter resistance.

Research has shown that, although some small doses of anxiety can increase performance, severe anxiety can decrease effectiveness of performance (Burton, 2010). What is anxiety? Studies have shown that anxiety is associated with abnormal gamma amino butyric acid (GABA) binding. GABA is usually released automatically when arousal reaches a certain level. It then binds with GABA receptors on excited neurons which underpins the experience of anxiety (Liddle, 2001). Research by Professor Robert Drugan (2000) has shown that animals who show resilience in the face of uncontrollable stress, have a unique pattern of GABA binding. They show increased gamma amino butyric acid (GABA) binding, a relaxed state and do not have as much emotional memory for the stressful occurrence. Animals that become helpless show decreased GABA activity and an accurate, emotional and powerful memory of the stressful occurrence. So, we need to build resilience. Surely though, to build resilience we need to expose our children to tasks where they can fail and learn?

Understanding Memory

'There are lots of people who mistake their imagination for their memory.'
– Josh Billings

We know what we saw. Don't we? Do you remember it like it was yesterday and could you tell the story like the back of your hand? We view the world through our own senses. Our eyes, ears, noses and skin. So the world is flat? Yes? It does beg the question, how do we really know that we are right? This has been the subject of films and plays for hundreds of years. I argue that the way we perceive much of our own lives is purely subjective. As Kathryn Schulz (2010) in *'Adventures In the Margin of Error'* exclaims:

> *"Failures of perception capture the essential nature of error. When we discover we have been wrong, we say that we were under an illusion, and when we no longer believe in something we say that we were disillusioned. People who possess the truth are perceptive, insightful, observant, illuminated, enlightened and visionary; by contrast the ignorant are in the dark." (P53)*

Many years ago people did believe their senses absolutely. Our memory is fallible and bias towards ourselves. Our reticular activating system or 'RAS' can be trained. It works a bit like a secretary in our heads deciding what is worth our attention and what is not. This is the reason why we don't remember things that are of no value to us.

Can you imagine if on an average 30 minute drive to work, we remembered *everything*: every colour we saw, every person's face, every turn, every note of the engine. It would drive us crazy. Our RAS exists to filter out what we don't need. Could it be that we are biased to see ourselves as perhaps, a bit better than we actually are? Our brains take short cuts. We have so much information to process these short cuts are called heuristics we make assumptions; we allocate certain stereotypes and have our own prejudices and viewpoints. In Biswas-Diener (2012), he describes one heuristic as representativeness. This is the basis of assumption, we make an assumption based on a representation. In education the assumptions that teachers make about pupils change and are often false, we need to make sure that as educators, we are in line with Carol Dweck's notion of the growth mindset.

Research has shown that the view of the self as good is partially determined by the way memory works. Memory is egocentric. Many people see themselves as responsible for good things such as passing an exam or helping someone and not responsible for bad things such as failure or hurting others (Carr, 2004). We process information according to our own self-schemas (set of our beliefs about ourselves, for example: if we use the memory of a student taking a test and then failing. If her self-schema is based around the notion that: 'I am a stupid child', the memory can be stored as: 'I tried my best and here is yet another example of how stupid I am'. We seem to be able to be able to add our own details, fill in the gaps, based on our own self-schemas. I argue that instances of positive failure will help develop an adaptive, positive, confident self-schema ready to deal with the future challenges a person has to face.

Doesn't it seem strange that some of our best ideas and solutions come to mind when engaging in absent-minded tasks: mowing the lawn, making the dinner, walking the dog? We don't seem to mind messing up at all when we are in private, when the situation is relaxed. How many of us, when learning how to work something, have a *test run* and make a complete mess out of it? Studies have shown that during these instances, there is a lot going on beneath the surface. Unconscious learning and absent-minded playing can lead to an increase in learning effectiveness.

This slow gradient of cognitive fitness seems to be especially effective for new, intricate practical solutions. This notion of 'relaxed trial and error' seems to have the best results (Berry and Broadbent, 1984). It seems to me, however, that the idea of relaxed trial and error has to be manufactured in lessons against the sociological culture of exam results, testing, sanctions and rewards. This is our natural default;

we were made to practically learn. It has even been proven by scientists that this kind of background learning is often more effective if you are not consciously concentrating (Claxton, 2008).

Motivation

'Why do I have to go to school? Because you do!'
– Anon

What motivates us? How are we motivated and can we cultivate it? How motivated are you to achieve your goals? Can you be bothered? What's the difference between being motivated and not? These are the kind of questions positive psychology attests to answer and begins by looking at goals.

One study conducted around goals found that people were much more likely to achieve their goals if those goals were intrinsic, internal and they were aligned with the person's core values, and developing interests, not dependant on a reward. The researchers even named this particular type of goal as self-concordant goals *(goals that are relevant and authentic to you)*. They also then discovered that when people did achieve these goals they were able to satisfy their own mental needs, were indeed happier and more fulfilled. They then went on to prove that people who had self-concordant goals reached them more often, recorded greater levels of well-being and were more satisfied with life than people who relied on rewards, sanctions, punishments and other extrinsic motivators (Sheldon and Elliot, 1999).

It is widely regarded in the field of Positive Psychology that intrinsic motivation is more beneficial that extrinsic. Intrinsic motivation is motivation that comes from inside you, rather than extrinsic motivation, which is being motivated by an external source such as a reward or punishment. Ryan and Deci (2000) describe how intrinsic motivation is strengthened by offering people choices, opportunities for self-direction and positive feedback.

However, they argue that feedback which indicates that negative performance has occurred weakens intrinsic motivation. I would argue that this is a temporary effect as long as the preconditions for positive failure are in place then it does very little damage indeed. Ryan and Deci describe how positive feedback was found to increase *perceived competence*. I believe negative feedback has its place. I argue that, in today's school system, negative feedback has its very own heterodoxy which is congruent with the failure heterodoxy.

Not only do we seem to be reluctant to give negative feedback, but Deci *et al* (1999) discovered that both punishment and rewards reduce intrinsic motivation and this is because they take away the notion of autonomy with the person. It is interesting to note that many UK and indeed western school systems predominantly focus on deferred gratification, rewards and punishments. Many students are becoming more and more grade focused. Research has shown that many students develop a particular attitude to their education that leads them to sacrifice their natural curiosity in order to learn for the test (Boaler, 1997). Studies have shown that in many cases children will learn how much it is possible to write in a few hours, what particular phrases or comments that will impress the examiner, revision techniques for the retention and regurgitation of facts and figures. These learning habits are tied to the tasks of passing exams and post university many do not engage in these again. (Entwistle, 1990 & Boaler, 1997).

When pupils are fully engaged they are difficult to get out of the classroom rather than in. This has been called powerful learning. Research has shown that powerful learners don't need much encouragement; they are learning because they want to. (I would argue they are often intrinsically motivated). Paradoxically, however, children who are praised and rewarded often become less creative and imaginative, confident to learn on their own. The external reward has killed the intrinsic satisfaction (Lepper and Greene,1988). I have seen in my experience pupils who sadly become addicted to praise. They have learned to learn for the external approval not for the intrinsic pleasure of succeeding in an endeavour.

The same has been shown to happen with real rewards and incentives. If you pay a child for attending school which they may well be enjoying anyway, then later stop the rewards or payment, often the enjoyment and motivation that was there in the beginning, is now gone. In addition there is a reluctance to engage. In congruence, Bronson (2007), in the *New York* magazine explains how young people who are consistently told that they are 'bright' or 'talented' adopt lower standards of success. I argue that if children are systematically praised for their ability, they will become more cautious, take less risks and fear failure far more than a child who achieved the task/exam/challenge against real standards and is praised over the effort invested in that particular endeavour.

Guy Claxton (2008) discusses how bland non-specific, unearned praise does not build self-esteem and how it can actually damage an educator's reputation as students then begin to disregard what they say. It has been categorically proven that intrinsically motivated people show more interest, confidence and excitement about the challenge or task they are internally motivated to do than those who are extrinsically motivated by, say, reward or punishment (Ryan and Deci, 2000).

SCHOOL EXAM QUESTION:
8. Name the successor of the first Roman Emperor.
Answer: The Second Roman Emperor.

Flow

"We are never more fully alive, more completely ourselves, or more deeply engrossed in anything than when we are playing."
– Charles Schaefer

Have you ever lost track of time during an activity because you are enjoying it so much? Begun a task and then got so engrossed the dinner burns, you miss an engagement or deadline? Recent research in positive psychology has defined this further being in a state of flow. Csikszentmihayli (1992) conceptualised it and it is further explained by Sarah Lewis (2011) in *'Positive Psychology at Work'*:

"The state experienced by people when they are so fully engaged and absorbed in what they are doing that time ceases to matter, any sense of self-consciousness or ego disappears and the person and the activity become as one." (P51-52)

Research that is being carried out is suggesting that this state is extremely constructive to learning. It seems that the world has vanished and really only when you cease experiencing flow, you know that you have been in it and the task you thought was meant to take 30 minutes has now taken three hours and you are completely fine with that! Ilona Boniwell (2006) who is a pioneer of positive psychology describes how flow happens under very specific conditions; when we encounter a challenge that is testing for our skills and yet our skills and capacities are such that we have just enough competency to meet this challenge. Additionally Seligman (2011) discusses how there are no easy roads to flow; he, in fact, mentions the opposite. It seems that to be fully engrossed in flow, you have to put into practice your best talents, skills and level of effort.

Studies show that by default we naturally look for and sometimes even create challenges, problems or issues that will stretch our competency and skill at reacting to new events (Meadows, 2006). We seem to be almost *programmed* to learn and practice. I argue we are also hard wired to fail, hard wired to learn through positive failure. It seems to just be a question of whether we allow ourselves to. Research shows that when we are relaxed and playing, we almost deliberately make mistakes, laughter is usually involved, and this pattern is repeated in nature, we want to see what happens (Clark & Karmiloff–Smith, 1993). We attempt to try our best not fail or make mistakes when the stakes are high. Using positive failure whilst learning will help prepare both, children and adults for high stake environments. I argue that the disposition to discover other possibilities, take risks, experiment or be creative, merges flexibility, adaptability, creativity with efficiency and logic.

Csiksentmihayli (1992) uses the phrase *'success in the process of achieving'* whilst describing flow. I believe this is what we should be measuring. No one leaves school an expert at anything and by encouraging perfectionist tendencies and over praising our children we seem to be fostering this misconception. I believe the real successes of school are the young adults who have got it wrong, yet taken and continue to take steps on their path of lifelong learning.

Csikzentmihayli (1992) came to the conclusion that flow is a universal experience, and it has several important characteristics that need to happen at the same time which included clarity of goals and immediate feedback, transformation of time and an intrinsic satisfaction.

Research shows that you seem to be almost absent of emotions during the experience. You are just very much getting on with it (Seligman, 2003). Ilona Boniwell (2006) believes that a fear of failure will also be absent during flow. I add to this that if one understands and employs the theory of positive failure it will enhance flow. Csikszentmihayli (1998) believes that successful students know the value of flow and find it pleasurable and satisfying putting in the effort to get their heads round a difficult idea. I argue that it is very important we cultivate more opportunities in schools and organisations for pupils/people to get into flow whilst learning. How do we do this? We need to look at flow in more detail. Here lies the true role of a good teacher. Breaking learning into goals which are achievable yet stretch and use skills that are relevant to the children, giving them the space to fail. Research shows that the tasks which lead us to flow must be achievable, must use our skill set to the limit and must include feedback.

If the challenge is too high or too difficult then students can stray into anxiety and become nervous, if it is too easy then students can stray into boredom (Carr, 2004). Tasks that lead to flow experiences have clear goals and feedback is immediate, not delayed. Feedback does not have to come from a teacher, for example, playing sports and scoring goals, climbing a mountain, flying a plane, these are all tasks where the feedback is immediate. During flow we cease to be self-aware. It seems that the only time we are jolted out of this is when we lose concentration, are in danger or we have an emotional reaction.

I argue that, failure in flow should be irrelevant to progress of the activity or task. If one fails in flow you shouldn't be jolted out because you are clear that you are learning and this is positive failure. If you start making people accountable for mistakes and failure whilst learning, there will be no flow, they will become self-critical because the goal has changed and is no longer about learning, it is to achieve the grade. The grade should be the by-product of learning not the sole purpose. Positive failure in flow should act as a catalyst for progression and achievement.

Positive Failure

Chapter **Four**
Failing is Learning

Positive Failure

Let us return to the theory of positive failure in more detail.

> **Positive failure:** is failure after appropriate investment that leads to further learning or development.

> **Negative failure:** is failure after inappropriate investment that stunts further progress or development.

Conducive to positive failure are appropriately supportive and forgiving relationships in an unforgiving environment. The more realistic and tangible the challenge or standard, the more likely it is for positive failure to occur.

I argue that negative failure adversely effects self-esteem and resilience. Unlike negative failure, positive failure can increase motivation and resilience and not only, does not adversely affect self-esteem, but strengthens and builds it. For positive failure to yield the best results, I suggest the following preconditions are important.

> **Preconditions for positive failure:** acceptance of one's own vulnerability, having a growth mindset and embracing imperfection.

> **Preconditions for negative failure:** defiance of one's own vulnerability, having a fixed mindset and embracing perfectionism.

Negative failure is very natural. When we refuse to learn, adapt, innovate and fail, we face the harshest type of failure. In the same widely accepted way as imperfection is the human default. The world does not care about our feelings. If we do not invest effort and simply do nothing, the world will not care for us. If we remain isolated and fool ourselves that the world is a forgiving environment and its okay that we didn't catch that food tonight, we will starve and die. We need to work to cultivate those appropriately supportive and forgiving relationships in our unforgiving world. In our history we often like to focus on the successes and the times we got it right, when sometimes we really need to look at our failures. Failure forces exploration, discovery and progression.

Negative failure has a similar psychological effect as the physical effect of smallpox in that it disables, de-motivates and isolates victims. We don't want to talk about it and are sometimes ashamed of it. I argue that if we do take this course, like a piece of food left in a dark, wet, warm place, it will fester and rot. Outside (and sometimes in) educational establishments, negative failure is just part of life. I argue that we are not effectively training our children how to deal with it. Unwillingly, teachers can inadequately prepare students for the natural, powerful experiences of negative failure without giving them many smaller exposures to positive failure building up their resilience.

It is also important to know when to abandon something. There is a time to cut and run. It takes courage to give up and walk away. Two researchers, Charles Carver and Michael Schier (2002), even go as far to argue that giving up is a human strength. They suggest that there are two clear pathways to giving up, the first is to let the goal go, the second to give up the effort. It seems that many people find themselves in a position where they are unwilling to give up the goal and instead sacrifice the effort. For example, the student who has chosen the easiest subject seems to lack in effort before they will give up the subject.

Uncharacteristically, I argue that a forgiving environment in learning can be negative. It is the *relationship* that needs to be forgiving. I argue that a supportive yet unforgiving environment is needed. Cameron *et al* (2003) describes how forgiveness is associated with broader and richer social relationships, a greater sense of empowerment, better health, faster recovery from disease, less depression and less anxiety. Do we really want our children empowered because they didn't try? Do we want them to be happy and not anxious that they failed? I argue that forgiveness is important within relationships, however, can be harmful in the process of failure.

For positive and negative failure to make sense, concrete, realistic and tangible standards have to be in place. It is no good failing against a false or over/under inflated standard as this is just a waste of time. In education, by lowering the standard we are not helping the students at all. Robinson (2009) describes how the problem is not that we aim too high and fail but aim too low and succeed.

I hypothesise that there is not enough exposure to positive failure at school and building the resilience of children, self-esteem has become a major issue. When children leave school and their resilience is tested by the inevitable exposure to negative failure, it seems that we see stagnant self-efficacy, a decrease in resilience and decreased self-esteem.

Positive failure is a vaccine; it is a process of psychological immunisation. It hurts, is unpleasant, and we naturally shy away from it. I argue that avoiding failure is responsible for the huge lack in resilience we have seen in many adolescents in western society.

The Preconditions for Positive and Negative Failure

I argue that the key to the dismantling of the *failure heterodoxy*, is to facilitate the pre-conditions for positive failure. The foundations of the failure heterodoxy are the pre-conditions for negative failure and they are making a great deal of money for a lot of people. The preconditions for negative failure are threefold: The first is invulnerability. I argue that being vulnerable is often perceived as being weak and this is a dangerous misconception. Being vulnerable is as uncomfortable as being imperfect. Yet, once a person has got their head round this, we can begin to positively fail.

Many of the great ideas, innovations and instances of progress have embodied the pre-conditions for positive failure. Being comfortable, invulnerable and perfect did not help us evolve into what we are today. Yet this is exactly what we seem to strive for. I argue that to fully embrace the concept of positive failure, one must be comfortable with one's own vulnerability. Research seems to show that we have a real issue with the fact that there are no guarantees in our lives and that we are anxious people, indeed many of us have little tolerance for vulnerability (Brown, 2010).

To embrace positive failure and to build around yourself the required preconditions is not an easy task. Brené Brown (2010) in *'The Gifts of Imperfection'* comments on joy:

> *"Joy is as thorny and as sharp as any of the dark emotions. To love someone fiercely, to believe in something with your whole heart, to fully engage in a life that doesn't come with guarantees – these are risks that involves vulnerability and often pain. When we lose our tolerance for discomfort, we lose joy. In fact, addiction research shows us that intensely positive experiences are just as likely to cause relapse as an intensely painful experiences."* (P73)

I argue that vulnerability and trust are conducive to positive failure. One definition of trust is conceptualised by Dunn and Schweitzer (2005), who describe how trust is the acceptance of vulnerability based upon positive expectations about another's behaviour. If we are not prepared to be vulnerable and trust others, it seems that it is much harder to engage in positive failure.

The second precondition of negative failure is having a fixed mindset. An example of a fixed mindset approach to ability, would be believing a child is 'bright' or 'stupid' and that intelligence is not changeable. It is synonymous with structures such as the 11+ exam, which exudes that students have a fixed amount of intelligence. Covington and Omelich (1979) describe how, although trying is important for success and is encouraged by teachers and parents, if the children try

59

and fail [with a fixed ability attitude], then it is difficult to escape the conclusion that they lack ability.

The third precondition for negative failure is perfectionism. I argue striving for perfection is foolish. Scott (2007) proved that perfectionism hampers success. He also found that it is often the path to depression, anxiety, addiction and life paralysis. Life paralysis refers to the opportunities and chances we have that we overlook because we are afraid that we aren't good enough. Imperfection through challenge seems to be a part of us, so why are we so obsessed with perfection? I argue that in the same way that success is paralysing, so is perfectionism. Brown (2010) comments on perfectionism and even refers to herself as a recovering perfectionist:

> "Where perfectionism exists, shame is always lurking; in fact, shame is the birthplace of perfectionism. Perfectionism is not the same thing as striving to be your best. Perfectionism is not about healthy achievement and growth. Perfectionism is the belief that if we live perfect, look perfect, and act perfect we can minimise or avoid the pain of blame, judgement and shame. It is a shield." (P56)

I argue that meaningful learning is a process and can be uncomfortable, risky and nerve wracking. By embracing our own imperfections and failing, it seems we can achieve the best results in the end. Rather than trying to live up to a perfectionist idea of ourselves, which is conceived by someone else or organisation, if you embrace your own strengths and also embrace your own weakness, as Lewis (2011) explains, you don't have to live up to this perfect ideal of yourself. I argue that perfectionism is perfectionism's undoing.

Positive Failure in Practice

Success through positive failure is mirrored in nature. I argue that the world as a whole is an unforgiving environment, instances of negative failure are much more common and potent than positive. However, it seems that positive failure developed as the most effective weapon against extinction. Organisms have established a range of different ways and instances where this can happen, almost 'against' nature. A study by Susan Rosenberg (2003) found that bacteria increased their mutation rates dramatically when confronted with the 'stress' of low energy supplies. When the pressure to exist, innovate and to discover a new way of surviving the bacteria begin to positively fail. They react to an unforgiving environment against tangible standards, deploying effort and thus leading to positive development. In congruence with this, Johnson (2010) explains how when the going gets tough, life tends to gravitate towards more innovative reproductive strategies. Even human sex and failure seem interconnected. Sex is positive failure. It embodies every precondition. Sex allows potentially useful innovations (DNA strains) to collide with other useful innovations. It embraces the vulnerability, imperfection and growth mindset of conception, and then often creates positive development.

It is not easy to operate virtuously, with an open willingness to show vulnerability and imperfection. However, I argue that when we do, our performance increases. Is positive failure more than increasing exceptional performance? Is it necessary for exceptional performance? Lewis (2011) highlights how the idea that generosity, forgiveness, appreciation, encouragement, and positive feedback are necessary to achieve high performance, is a radical thought, especially when times are tough. It can be tempting to be invulnerable, perfectionist and fixed to 'weather the storm' when maybe, as with a hurricane we need to be more vulnerable and open our windows.

What seems to be happening in many schools is that failure is demonised or disguised like a dirty secret, thus meaning that students are in for a heavy dose of negative failure, when they leave. I argue that this is demoralising, disabling and promoting the self-justification and defence mechanisms needed to justify failure at a cost to further learning and development. Yankelovich and Furth (2005) in their research have categorically found that the public in the west has a major distrust in our major institutions; however, below the cynicism we want honesty, transparency and integrity.

Another example is the incubator that was designed to positively fail by accepting vulnerability and embracing imperfection. This incubator was designed with an understanding that it would fail. Steven Johnson (2010) in his book 'Where Good Ideas Come From' explains:

> "Over one hundred infants per thousand still die in Liberia and Ethiopia, many of them premature babies that would have survived with access to incubators, but modern incubators are complex, expensive things. A standard incubator in an American hospital costs over $40,000. But the expense is arguably the smaller hurdle to overcome. Complex equipment breaks, and when it breaks you need the technical expertise and the specialist parts to fix it and you need the replacement parts. In the year that followed the 2004 Indian Ocean tsunami, the Indonesian city of Meulaboh received eight incubators from a range of international relief organisations. By late 2008 when MIT professor Tim Prestero visited the hospital, all eight were out of order from power surges and tropical humidity, along with the staff's inability to read the English repair manual. Some studies suggest that up to 95% of medical technology donated to developing countries breaks within the first five years of use." (P27)

The environment was invulnerable, 'perfect' and fixed. It was also morally isolated in that there was no way that the doctors and nurses could hold accountability to a gift. This state of affairs led to a stagnant self-efficacy, decreases resilience and decreased self-esteem. Johnson continues:

> *"Designing an incubator for a developing country wasn't just a matter of creating something that worked; it was also a matter of designing something that would break in a non-catastrophic way. You couldn't guarantee a steady supply of spare parts, or trained technicians. So Prestero and his team decided to build it with parts that were already abundant in the developing world. The idea had originated with a Boston doctor named Jonathon Rosen. They made an incubator out of automobile parts." (P28)*

The incubator could be powered by an adapted cigarette lighter; it used sealed beam headlights for warmth and so on. The incubator now held all the elements of positive failure. After a considerable investment of effort in the design process, they had created an appropriately supportive network in an unforgiving environment against tangible standards. This led to positive development, more babies surviving, Increasing self-esteem and self-efficacy. The doctors now are much more motivated, and open communication between them is much higher, as opposed to the isolated $40,000 incubators that now lie useless.

I argue that positive failure develops competence. I believe intelligence is linked to developing competence. Robert Sternberg's *Intelligence, Competence and Expertise*, in Elliot and Dweck (2005) offers a view of intelligence as relating to competence. He says that intelligence represents a set of developing competencies, and in turn these represent expertise. He describes experts as people who have developed their competence to a high level. Lauren Resnick (1999) describes intelligence as the habit of persistently trying to understand things and make them function better. I argue that intelligence is adaptability utilising appropriate resources. Following this train of thought, is it possible that positive failure increases competence, and by proxy intelligence?

What about when it really matters? When the consequences of failure are life and death. Even here, the key is making the supportive relationships and systems against the unforgiving environment by understanding that we are vulnerable and imperfect and crucially, that we get it wrong. Research shows that in organisations where the risks are great such as in the worlds of medicine and the emergency services where mistakes can be fatal. This is accepted, there are preconditions and systems in place to deal with failure. Mistakes are viewed as a ruthless audit (Weick and Sutcliffe, 2007).

Positive failure seems to have its best results when the learners/participants are ambivalent during the process. It seems that a lack of emotion is desirable. Schulz (2010) explains how there is no experience of being wrong, there is an experience of realising that we are wrong. She then explains how there is one particular feeling we seem to experience in the realization, it feels like being right.

Another example of positive failure is in the system of LCES detailed by Sarah Lewis (2011) in *'Positive Psychology at Work'*:

> *"LCES stands for lookouts, communication links, escape routes and safety zones. It is derived from the study of effective fire fighting in difficult situations. Communication links are clear; the group also identifies and keeps re-identifying as things change: their escape routes, at least two, in case of emergency; and the safety zone that is known to everyone that they can retreat to review the situation and communicate with each other." (P98)*

These structures support effective, ambivalent, adaptive behaviour in an extremely unforgiving environment. These examples of introducing positive failure into a very high risk and high consequence environment prove that positive failure is highly effective and that positive failure may have benefits in other systems, organisations and groups outside schools and learning institutions.

Throughout history, where there are significant human advances, there seems to be positive failure woven into the back story. None so much as in the field of Science. Stigler (1990) explains how the French mathematician and astronomer Pierre–Simon Laplace refined the theory of the distribution of errors, illustrated by the now familiar bell-curve. This theory was a way of displaying data that would not make sense if each piece was taken individually or some were inaccurate. It is also known as the *error curve*. This is significant for positive failure as this theory improved accuracy by allowing for and using failure and error. Laplace realised that you should try to get more error; collect enough flawed data, and there is a glimpse of the truth.

The genius of statistics as Laplace defined it was that it did not ignore errors; it quantified them. This to me is the single most influential breakthrough in realising that within learning, positive failure is a tool for development and should not be shunned and avoided. As opposed to being forced to think outside the box, when we begin to think inside the box rather than being fixated with success we may just start getting it right. As Menand (2002) observed; the right answer is, in a sense, a function of the [our] mistakes.

How Positive Failure Links in with Positive Psychology: An Overview

'Perhaps the history of the errors of mankind, all things considered, is more valuable and interesting than that of their discoveries.'
– Benjamin Franklin

Once you are right or correct, that's it, the end. It is about as fixed as it is possible to be. What if you're wrong? Johnson (2010) describes how being correct is like the phase – lock states of the human brain, all the neurons firing in perfect synchrony. And a world of complete failure would be unmanageable. In trying to define failure the contexts and subjective variables are almost infinite. It would almost have to be a working title, a truth or definition that will do for now. I suggest that the theory of positive and negative failure abandons being right and wrong and is almost more of a technique or learning mantra.

I argue that positive failure fosters self-efficacy and builds self-esteem. I also argue that the answer to raising children's self-esteem is to concentrate on creating supportive relationships in unforgiving *real environments* where they can develop the resilience needed to survive the inevitable negative failure they will encounter once they leave school. Self-efficacy was originally conceptualised and defined by Bandura and Walters (1963). It is primarily about confidence. Lutherans *et al* (2007) describe self-efficious people as welcoming new challenges that stretch their experience base. I hypothesise that positive failure in domains of weakness will build resilience and strength; positive failure in areas of strength will build competence. Biswas-Diener (2012) beautifully suggests that one attitude to small-stake mistakes is to embrace them as if they were your friends and also gateways to creativity, confidence and spontaneity. He talks about them as a learning and growth opportunity.

Lewis (2011) believes resilience is developed through repeated exposure to gradually increasing difficulties from which people learn in a productive way. I hypothesise that negative failure will foster hopelessness. Snyder (2000) believes that hope is strongest when it entails valued goals, and that there is an intermediate probability of attaining them due to challenging but not insurmountable obstacles. By employing the theory of positive failure, we can help children to not see their obstacles as insurmountable.

French Philosopher Henri Bergson (1956) hoped to provide his readers with a practical, intimate, acquaintance, with error similar to that of a partner or long-term companion. He believed that for better or for worse, error is our lifelong companion.

We hope of our children that they reach the highest heights. We push them and support them in every way we know how. Some will reach world-class performance levels. I argue that without positive failure, one will not arrive at world-class performance. You will fail on journeys such as this and occasionally individuals make it through the myriad of negative failure around them, however more often than not, behind the scenes are instance after instance of positive failure. It doesn't happen overnight. Clifton and Nelson (1992) studied just how long on average it takes talented individuals to arrive at world-class performance and found it to be between 10 – 17 years. Any good sports coach, musician or educationalist knows that to get it right, you have to get it wrong.

Positive Failure

Chapter **Five**
Conclusion

I asked the questions in *Positive Psychology at Work*, Lewis (2011): have we found ourselves teaching to compete rather than co-operate? To think narrowly, rather than broadly? To be frightened of uncertainty and the risk of error that accompanies it?

I think we have. We all know that everyone makes mistakes and we need to stop ignoring them and covering them up. We need to face facts. Me, you and millions before us fail and it is the essence of learning. In this age of accountability, to achieve the best performance and to really succeed we need to stop seeing failure as holding us back and use it to propel us forward. The need is more pressing than it has ever been. If we do not address this barrier to learning that is stealthily persuading our own children that they, themselves are failures and rejects, I believe that we face for the first time in human evolution, going backwards.

I believe the stage is now set to work on a new paradigm in education. I also argue that there is a foreboding sense of urgency to face our natural instincts and meet failure head on. We cannot afford to let it hold our schools, teachers and children back any longer. Rather than wasting time with small interventions and initiatives, if we embrace positive failure, we can then use it as a catalyst for trying new methods. Let's fail forward together, towards success.

We have tried throughout history to eradicate failure, error and imperfection with disastrous consequences – the Titanic; the perfect ship that would not sink; the Aryan 'perfect' race of the Nazis. We failed to understand failure itself. Science offers us the most useful example of positive failure. The idea behind the scientific method is that, observation leads to hypothesis from which one then experiments and finally evaluates. Blindingly simple. As we have seen, we all naturally want to verify our own ideas and beliefs; it is often the Scientists, Psychologists and Mathematicians who seem to seek as a collective to disprove, to find failure and to move step by step towards the truth.

We as human beings want to make sense of, discover, map and quantify our world. To do that we need to fail. Research shows that to actually make sense of something, it is an on-going process of forming and evaluating hypothesis, adjustment and open evaluation (Weick, 2006).

I do not wish to discount negative failure, and of course one can still learn from negative failure, but the risk of experiencing de-motivation, isolation and a reluctance to re-apply oneself will be prevalent, in addition to other dangerous consequences. Together positive and negative failure enable us to understand the mechanics of error. I hypothesise that both positive and negative failure have the power to turn virtue into vice and vice-versa. They are raw constructs of nature and as such need to be respected. For children and young adults in learning environments, positive failure is key to the success we seem to crave for our children.

I argue that real experts understand that experts are never really experts. Individuals are constantly in a process of developing expertise when they work with a given domain. Once one is presented as an expert, it suggests a fixed belief, a rule, a decision or something *in stone*. It also creates a somewhat *failure lust* from others. It greatly increases the probability of encountering negative failure. In contrast by adapting a malleable, growth mindset and finding ways to ask questions as opposed to making statements seems to bind teams, make great leadership and, applied appropriately, enable progression. It has been proved that practical wisdom leads to operating in the master virtue of resilience and I argue positive failure cultivates practical wisdom. There is much work to be done around positive failure, however, the evidence does show that its core characteristics are similar to *phronesis* and cultivate psychological strength, a growth mindset which over time sets a trajectory towards operating in *the master virtue of resilience*.

Rather than trying to live up to a perfectionalist idea of yourself, which is projected by someone else, if we embrace our own strengths and also embrace our own weakness, as Lewis (2011) explains, we don't have to live up to this perfect ideal of ourselves. As Schulz (2010) suggests, we should foster an intimacy with our own fallibility. I argue that failure is essential to who we are, I also encourage us to see failure as a gift, as an irreplaceable source of laughter, art, individuality, creativity and change.

Schools and educational establishments are stretched across the world to breaking point. I believe that we cannot afford to let any more children be lost to the relentless testing and pursuit of excellence and perfectionism. We are failing to learn and we need to learn how to positively fail. Failure will always be unpleasant. I argue that we should be cultivating positive failure in learning to enable us to cope with the inevitable negative failure later in life and thus aiming towards a *failure immunity* achieved by multiple instances of positive failure. Isn't it better to be daring, bold and adventurous? Weren't we designed to explore and discover? Have we not achieved tremendous feats of engineering, creativity, art and progression? Aren't we the most advanced species on the planet? Isn't love the most powerful force on earth? We did not get this far by being timid, cautious, right, successful and obedient. Positive failure is quintessentially human. We are all only here for a short while, the next century will bring its own challenges and rather than thinking we have all the answers, let's get it wrong, let's progress, let's achieve and let's fail – together.

Positive Failure

Bibliography

Abramson, L., Alloy, L., Hankin, B., Clements, C., Zhu, L., Hogan, M. and Whitehouse, W. (2000). Optimistic cognitive style and invulnerability to depression. In J. Gillham (ed.) *The Science of Optimism and Hope* (pp. 75 – 98). Philadelphia, PA: Templeton Foundation Press.

Aldrich, R., An Introduction to the History of Education, in Claxton, G. (2008) *What's the Point of School?*. (p37) UK: Oneworld Publications.

Algoe, S., Haidt, J. & Gable, S. (2008). Beyond reciprocity: Gratitude and relationships in everyday life. *Emotion*, Vol 8(3), pp. 425-429.

Andrews, R. & Torgerson, J. *et al*(2006). The effect of Grammar Teaching on writing development. *British Educational Research Journal*, 32 (1) pp. 39 – 55

Arnott, A. (2011). The Space to Fail. In S, Lewis (Eds) (2011) *Positive Psychology at Work: How Positive Leadership and Appreciative Inquiry Create Inspiring Organizations*. Chichester: Wiley & Blackwell.

Aronson, J., Fried, C. & Good, C. (2002). Reducing the effects of stereotype threat on African American college students by shaping theories of intelligence. *Journal of Experimental Social Psychology*, 38, pp 113–125.

Balchin, T., et al (2008). *The Routledge Companion to Gifted Education*. London: Routledge.

Bandura, A. & Walters, R. (1963). *Social Learning and Personality Development*. New York: Holt, Rinehart and Winston.

Bannerman, C., Soafer, J. & Watt, J. (2006). *Creative Gliding Space in Navigating the unknown*. Middlesex: University Press London.

Bartlett, M. & De Steno, D. (2006). Gratitude and Prosocial Behaviour, Helping when it costs you. *Psychological Science*. Boston MA. Vol. 17. No. 4 pp 319-325.

Baumeister, R., Bratslavsky, E., Finkenauer, C. & Vohs, K. (2001). Bad is stronger than good. *Review of General Psychology*, 5, pp323-370.

Baumeister, R.,et al (2003). Psychological Science in the Public interest, 4, (pp.1 – 44). In G, Claxton. (2008). *What's the point of school?*.UK: Oneworld Publications.

Baumeister, R., Campbell, J., Krueger, J. & Vohs, K., (2003). Does high self-esteem cause better performance, interpersonal success, happiness or healthier lifestyles? *Psychological Science in the Public Interest*, 4(1).

Beare, H. (2006). *How We envisage Schooling in the 21st Century*. London:SSAT.

Beck, A. (1976). *Cognitive Therapy and the Emotional Disorders*. New York: International Universities Press.

Becker, E. (1973). *Denial of Death*. New York: Free Press.

Ben-Shahar, Tal. (2007). *Happier: Learn the secrets to daily Joy and Lasting Fulfilment*. USA: MCGraw Hill Companies. pp 92- 143.

Bergson, H. (1956). *Laughter, Essay on Comedy*. Doubleday and Company Inc. Wylie Sypher, P61.

Berry, D. & Broadbent, D. (1984). On the relationship between task performance and associated verbalized knowledge. *Quarterly Journal of Experimental Psychology*. 36A, pp. 209 – 31.

Bettenson, H. (2003). *The City of God*. UK: Penguin.

Birney, R., Burdick, H. & Teevan, R. (1969). *Fear of Failure*. New York: Van Nostrand Reinhold.

Biswas-Diener, R. (2012). *The Courage Quotient*. San Fransisco: Jossey-Bass – A Wiley Imprint.

Blackmore, S. (1999). *The Meme Machine*. UK: Oxford University Press.

Blakemore, S. & Frith, U. (2005). *The Learning Brain*, USA: Blakewell Publishing.

Blackwell, L., Trzesniewski,K. & Dweck,C. (2007). Implicit theories of intelligence predict achievement across an adolescent transition: A longitudinal study and intervention. *Child Development*, 78, pp 246–263.

Block, J.H. & Block, J. (1980). The role of ego-control and ego –resiliency in the organization of behaviour. In W.A. Collins (Ed), *Minnesota symposia on child psychology* (Vol. 13, pp. 39 – 101). Hillsdale, NJ: Erlbaum.

Blum ,J. (1978). *Pseudoscience and mental ability: The Origins and Fallacies of the IQ controversy.* New York: Monthly Review Press.

Boaler, J. (1997). When even the winners are losers: evaluating the experience of 'top set' students. *Journal of Curriculum Studies*, 29 (2) pp. 165-182.

Boniwell, I. (2006) *Positive Psychology in a Nutshell, A Balanced introduction to the science of optimal functioning.* UK: PWBC.

Bourdieu, P. (1992). *Outline of a Theory of Practice*, Cambridge, England: Cambridge University Press.

Bowlby, J. (2005). *A Secure Base: Clinical Applications of Attachment Theory*, UK, USA & Canada: Routledge.

Brickman , P. & Campbell, D. (1971). Hedonic relativism and planning the good society. In M. Appley (ed). *Adaption-level Theory* (pp 287–305). New York: Academic Press.

Brickamn, P., Coates, D. & Janoff –Bulman, R. (1978). Lottery winners and accident victims: Is happiness relative?. *Journal of Personality and Social Psychology*, 36, pp. 917–927.

Brighouse, T. (2006). *Essential pieces, the jigsaw of a successful school*, UK: Research Machines plc.

Brighouse, T., (2006). *How successful head teachers survive and thrive, Four phases of headship, Five uses of time, Six essential tasks and seven ways to hold onto your sanity.* UK: Research Machines plc. Copyright Tim Brighouse.

Briner, R. & Dewberry, C. (2007). *Staff well being is key to school success.* UK: Department.

Bristow, M., Ireson, G. & Coleman,A. (2007). A life in the day of a head teacher, A study of practice and well-being. *The Practitioner Report*, UK: National college for school leadership.

Bronson, P. (2007). *How not to talk to your kids.* USA: New York Magazine, 20/02/2007.

Brown, B. (2007) *I Thought It Was Just Me (but it isn't): Telling the Truth About Perfectionism, inadequacy and Power.* New York: Penguin/Gotham books.

Brown, B. (2010). *The Gift Of imperfection – Let Go Of Who You're Supposed To Be And Embrace Who You Are.* USA. Hazeldon.

Burton, N., (2010) *The Art of Failure, The Anti Self Help Guide,* UK: Acheron Press.

Buss, D. (2000). The Evolution Of Happiness. *American Psychologist* 55: pp.15–23.

Cameron, K,. Dutton, J., and Quinn, R. (Eds). (2003). *Positive Organizational Scholarship: Foundations of a New Discipline.* San Fransisco: Berrett – Koehler.

Cameron, K., Bright, D., and Caza, A. (2004). Exploring the relationships between organizational virtuousness and performance. *American Behavioural Scientist.* 47 (6) : 766 – 790

Carr, A. & Wilde, G. (1988). Effects of actual and potential stressor control on physiological and self- reported stress responses. *Journal of Social and Clinical Psychology* 6 (3 / 4): pp. 371-87.

Carr, A. (2004). *Positive Psychology: The science of happiness and Human strengths.* USA, UK & Canada: Routledge.

Carr, M. (2000). *Assessment in Early Childhood Settings: Learning Stories.* London: Paul Chapman.

Carver, C.S. & Scheier, M. (2002). Three human strengths. In L. Aspinwall & U. Staudinger (Eds), *A psychology of human strengths* (pp. 87 – 102). Washington, DC: American Psychological Association.

Clark, A. & Karmiloff–Smith, A. (1993). 8, (4) *The cognizer's innards: a psychological and philosophical perspective on the development of thought.* Mind and Language, pp. 487–519.

Claxton, G. (2008). *What's the Point of School?.* UK: Oneworld Publications.

Clifton, D.O. & Harter, J.K. (2003). Investing in Strengths. In A. K.S. Cameron, B. J.E. Dutton & C. R.E. Quinn (Eds.), *Positive Organizational Scholarship* (pp. 111-121). San Francisco: Berrett-Koehler Publishers, Inc

Clifton, D. & Nelson, P. (1992). *Soar With Your Strengths.* New York. Dell.

Coffield, F,. Moseley, D *et al* (2004). *Learning styles and pedagogy in post 16 learning: a systematic and critical review.* UK: Learning and Skills Research Centre.

Cole, D., Maxwell, S. & Martin, J. (1997). Reflected self-appraisals: Strength and structure of the relation of teacher, peer, and parent ratings to children's self-perceived competencies. *Journal of Educational Psychology*, Vol 89(1), pp. 55-70.

Collishaw, S., Maughan, B., Goodman, R. & Pickles, A. (2004). Time trends in adolescent mental health. *Journal of Child Psychology and Psychiatry.* 45 (8). pp. 1350–62.

Connors, J., Maisto, S. and Zywiak (1998). Male and Female Alcoholics, Attributions Regarding the Onset and Termination of Relapses and the Maintenance of Abstinence. *Journal of Substance Abuse*, 10. No. 1 27 – 42.

Costa, A. & Kallick, B. (2000). *Discovering and Exploring Habbits of Mind.* Vancouver: Association for supervision and Curriculum Development.

Covington, M. (1992). *Making the Grade: A self-worth perspective on motivation and school reform.* New York: Cambridge University Press.

Covington, M. & Amelich, C. (1979). Effort: The double-edged sword in school achievement. *Journal of Educational Psychology*, 71, pp. 169–182.

Craig, C. (2007). *The potential dangers of a systematic, explicit approach to teaching social and emotional skills (SEAL).* Centre for Confidence and Well Being.

Craig, C. (2009). Lecture at The University Of East London.

Crooker, J. & Park, L. (2004). The Costly Pursuit of Self Esteem. *Psychological Bulletin.* 130: pp. 392–414.

Csikszentmihayli, M. (1992). *Flow – The classic work on how to achieve happiness.* USA: Harper and Row.

Dawkins, R. (1996). *The Selfish Gene.* UK: Oxford University Press.

Deakin-Crick, R., Broadfoot, P. & Claxton, G. (2004). Developing an effective lifelong learning inventory: The ELLI Project. *Assessment in Education.* 11 (3), pp. 247-72.

Department for Education and Skills. (2007). *Social and Emotional Aspects of Learning for Secondary Schools (SEAL)*: Guidance booklet. pp 5-8

Department for Children, Schools and Families. (2008). SFR 10/2008. School workforce in England. http://www.dcsf.gov.uk/rsgateway/DB/SFR/s000787/SFR10_2008.pdf

Delle Fave, A. & Massimini, F. (2003). Optimal experience in work and leisure among teachers and physicians: individual and bio-cultural implications. *Leisure Studies*, 22, pp 323-342.

Diener, E. (2003). What is positive about positive psychology: the Curmudgeon and Pollyana. *Psychological Inquiry*, 14, 115 – 120, p 117.

Diener, M.L. & Lucas, R. E. (2004). Adults' desires for children's emotions across 48 countries: Associations with individual and national characteristics. *Journal of Cross-Cultural Psychology*, 35(5), 525 -547

Dillon, J. (1990). *The Practice of Questioning.* London:Routledge.

Drugan, R. (2000). The neurochemistry of stress resilience and coping: a quest for natures own antidote to illness. In J. Gillham (ed). *The Science of Optimism and Hope* (pp. 57 – 71). Philadelphia, PA: Templeton Foundation Press.

Duckworth, A. & Seligmann, M. (2005). Self-Discipline outdoes IQ in predicting academic performance of adolescents. *Psychological Science.* 16 (12), pp. 939–44.

Dunn, J.,& Schweitzer, M. (2005). Feeling and Believing: The Influence of Emotion on Trust. *Journal of Personality and Social Psychology.* Vol 88(5). pp. 736-748.

Dweck, C. (1999). *Self theories: Their role in Motivation, Personality and Development.* London: Psychology Press.

Dweck, C. (2007). *Mindset: The New Psychology of Success*. New York: Ballantine Books.

Dweck, C. (2010). Mindsets and equitable education. Principal leadership, http://www.rippowammiddle.org/Site_2/Parent_Links_files/Mindsets%20%26%20Equitable%20Education.pdf.

Ehrenreich, B. (2009). *Brightsided: How The Relentless Promotion of Positive Thinking Has Undermined America*. New York: Metropolitan Books.

Elliot, A. & Dweck, C. (2005). *Handbook of Competence and Motivation*, New York: Guildford Press.

Ellis, A. & Harper, R. (1975). *A New Guide to Rational Living*, North Hollywood, CA: Wiltshire.

Entwistle, N. (1990). *Styles of Learning and Teaching*. New York: Beekman Books.

Festinger, L. (1957). *A Theory of Cognitive Dissonance*. USA: Stanford University Press.

Fitzpatrick, D., In R, Jones (1995). Smart brains: neuroscientists explain the mystery of what makes us human. *American School Board Journal*, 182 (11), pp. 22 – 26.

Fowers, B.J. (2005). *Virtue and psychology: Pursuing excellence in ordinary practices*. Washington, DC: American Psychological Association.

Friedrick, S. & Lowenstein, G. (1999). Hedonic adaptation. In E Kahneman, E. Diener and N. Scwartz (eds), *Well-being: The Foundations of Hedonic Psychology*. (pp. 302 – 29). New York: Russel Sage Foundation.

Fredrickson, B. & Losada, M. (2005). *Positive affect and the complex dynamics of human flourishing*. American Psychologist, 60, pp 678 -686.

Frome, P. & Eccles, J. (1998). Parents influence on children's achievement-related perceptions. *Journal of Personality and Social Psychology*. 74, pp. 435 – 52.

Gardener, H. (1983/1993). *Frames of Mind: Theory of Multiple Intelligences*. New York: Basic Books.

Gardener, H. (2000). *Intelligence Reframed: Multiple intelligences for the 21st century.* New York: Basic Books.

Garmezy, N. (1991). Resilience in children's adaptation to negative life events and stressed environments. *Pediatric Annals,* 20, 459 – 466.

Gerhardt, S. (2010). *The Selfish Society: How we all forgot to love one another and made money instead.* UK: Simon and Schuster ltd.

Gibbs, N. (1995). *The EQ factor: new brain research suggests that emotions, not IQ, may be the true measure of human intelligence.* USA: Time Magazine.

Gilbert, J. (2005). *Catching the Knowledge Wave? The Knowledge Society and the Future of Education.* Wellington: New Zealand Council for Educational Research Press.

Gillham, J. (2000). *The Science of Optimism and Hope.* Philadelphia, PA: Templeton Foundation Press.

Good, C.,Aronson, J. & Inzlicht, M. (2003). Improving adolescents' standardized test performance: An intervention to reduce the effects of stereotype threat. *Applied Developmental Psychology,* 24, pp 645–662.

Goleman, D. (1996). *Emotional Intelligence: Why it can Matter More than IQ.* London: Bloomsbury Publishing.

Gough, H. (1991). *Scales and Combinations of Scales: What do they tell us and what do they mean?.* Paper presented at the 99th Annual convention of the American Psychological Assocation, San Fransisco, August 1991, Data obtained by Twenge, J. in 2001.

Gollwitzer, P. & Wicklund, R. (1985). The pursuit of self-defining goals. In J. Khul and J. Beckmann (Eds.), *Action control: From cognition to behaviour,* pp. 61 – 85. Heidelberg: Springer –Verlag.

Graham, S. (1991). Communicating Low ability in the classroom: Bad things good teachers sometimes do. In S. Graham and V. Folkes (Eds), *Attribution theory: Applications to achievevment, mental health and interpersonal conflict.* (pp. 17 – 36) NJ: Hillsdale, Erlbaum.

Gray, J.R., Braver, T.S. & Raichle , M.E. (2002). Integration of emotion and cognition in the lateral prefrontal cortex. *PNAS*, 99 (6), 4115 – 4120.

Hadot, P. (2002). *What is Ancient Philosophy?* Cambridge, MA: Harvard University Press.

Greene, R.R. (2003). Resilience theory: theoretical and professional conceptualizations. *Journal of Human Behaviour in the Social Environment*, 8 (4), 75 – 91.

Haidt, J. (2006). *The Happiness Hypothesis.* USA: Basic Books.

Hargreaves, D. (2004). *About Learning: Report of The Learning Working Group.* London: Demos.

Hebb, D. (1949). The Organization of behaviour. New York: Wiley. A more recent exposition can be found in; Spitzer, M. (1999). *The Mind Within the Net*, Cambridge MA: MIT Press.

Hewitt, J. (1998). *The Myth of Self Esteem.* New York: St Martins Press. p51.

Holloway, S. (1988). Concepts of Ability and Effort in Japan and the United States. *Review of Educational Research.* Vol. 58. No 3. Pp. 327 -345.

House of Commons Children, Schools and Families Committee. (2008). Testing and Assessment. *Third Report of Session 2007-08.* Vol I. (HC 169-1). House of Commons, London. The Stationery Office Ltd.

Irvine, M. (2005). Young labeled 'Entitlement Generation'. AP June 2005, in Twenge, J. (2006). *Generation Me.* New York: Free Press, a division of Simon and Schuster Inc.

James, W. (1880). *Great Men, Great Thoughts, and the Environment.* Boston: Houghton Mifflin.

Jaycox, L., Seligmann, M., Reivich, K. & Gillham, J. (1994). Prevention of depressive symptoms in school children. *Behaviour research and therapy* 32: pp. 374 – 60.

Johnson, S. (2010). *Where Good Ideas Come From –The Natural History of Innovation.* UK: Allen Lane.

Joseph, S. & Linley, P. (2005). Positive Adjustment to Threatening Events: An Organismic Valuing Theory of Growth Through Adversity. *Review of General Psychology*, Vol 9(3), pp. 262-280.

Joseph, S,. & Linley, P. (2005). The Human Capacity for Growth Through Adversity: *American Psychologist*, Vol 60(3), pp. 262-264.

Joseph, S. & Linely, A. (2008). *Trauma, Recovery and Growth, Positive psychological perspectives on post traumatic stress*. UK: John Wiley and sons.

Kagen, J. (1994). *Galen's Prophecy: Temprement in Human Nature*. New York: Basic Books.

Kanner , A. & Gomes, M. (1995). The all-consuming self. In T. Roszak, M.E Gomes and A. D Kanner (Eds), *Ecopsychology: restoring the Earth, healing the mind* (pp. 77 – 91). San Francisco: Sierra Club Books.

Kasser, T. (2002). *The High Price of Materialism*. Cambridge MA: MIT Press.

Kashdan, T. (2009). *Curious? Discover the missing ingredient to a fulfilling life*. New York: Morrow.

Kernis, M. & Paradise, A. (2002). Distinguishing between secure and fragile forms of high self-esteem. In Deci, E., and Ryan, R. *Handbook of self-determination research*, pp.339 – 360. New York, Rochester: University of Rochester Press.

Kohut, H. (1971). *The analysis of the self.* New York: International Universities Press.

Kramer, R. (1991). *Ed School Follies: The Miseducation of America's Teachers*. New York: Free Press. p 33.

Kumar, S. & Jagacinski, C. (2006). Imposters have goals too: the imposter phenomenon and its relationship to achievement goal theory. *Personailty and Individual Differences*, 40, pp. 147–157.

Langer, E. (1975). The illusion of control. *Journal of Personality and Social Psychology* 32: pp. 311 – 28.

Le Doux, J. (1999). *The Emotional Brain*. London: Phoenix.

Lepper, M. & Greene, D. (1988). *The Hidden Cost of Reward*. New Jersey: Lawrence Erlbaum.

Lewis, S. (2011). *Positive Psychology at Work: How Positive Leadership and Appreciative Inquiry Create Inspiring Organizations*. Chichester: Wiley & Blackwell.

Liddle, P. (2001). *Disordered Mind and Brain*. London: Gaskell.

Linely, A. (2008). *Average to A* - Realising strengths in yourself and others*. UK: CAPP press.

Lutherans, F., Youssef, C., and Avolio, B. (2007). *Psychological Capital: Developing The Human Capital Edge*. Oxford: Oxford University Press.

Maddi, S.R. (2006). Hardiness: The courage to grow from stresses. *The Journal of Positive Psychology*, 1 (3), pp 160 – 168.

Mahonney, M. (1991). *Human Change Processes: The Scientific Foundation of Psychotherapy*. New York: Basic Books.

Marley, D. (2009). Five fold leap in the number of heads sacked. *The Times Education Supplement*, Section 2. 6/4/09.

Marshall, H. (1990) Beyond the workplace metaphor: The Classroom as a learning setting. *Theory into Practice*. USA: Taylor and Francis ltd: (29),2, pp. 94-101.

Maslow, A.H. (1965). *Eupsychian management: A journal*. New York: Richard D. Irwin.

Maslow, A.H. (1987). *Motivation and personality* (3rd ed.). New York: Harper Collins.

Matlin, M. & Stang, D. (1978). *The Pollyana Principle*. Cambridge, MA: Schenkman.

Matthews, G., Zeidner, M. & Roberts, R. (2004). *Emotional Intelligence: Science and Myth*, Cambridge, USA: MIT Press.

Mayer, J. & Salovey, P., et al. (1990). Perceiving affective content in ambiguous visual stimuli: a component of emotional intelligence. *Journal of Personality Assessment* 54: pp. 772 – 81.

Mayer, J., (1999). Emotional intelligence: popular or scientific psychology? in Monitor on Psychology, September, American Psychological Association Sternberg (ed.), *Handbook of Intelligence.* pp 396-420, UK: Cambridge University Press.

Mayer, J.D., Caruso, D. & Salovey, P. (2002). Emotional Intelligence and Emotional Leadership in R. Riggio & S. Murphy (Eds.), *Multiple Intelligences and Leadership.* Mahaw, NJ: Erlbaum.

McLaughlin, C. (2008). *Emotional well-being and its relationship to schools and classrooms: a criticial reflection:*, 36,4, pp 353 – 366, UK: Taylor and Francis: Routledge

Mc William, E. (2002). *How to Survive Best Practice.* Sydney: University of New South Wales Press.

Meadows, S. (2006). *The Child as a Thinker*, London: Routledge.

Mennand, L. (2002). The Genius of Statistics, The Metaphysical Club: A Story of Ideas in America, as found in Schulz, K. (2010) *Being Wrong, Adventures In The Margin Of Error.* UK: Portobello books.

Michalos, A. (1985). Multiple discrepancies theory (MDT). *Social Indicators Research* 16: pp. 347 – 413.

Miller, A. (1981). *The drama of the gifted child.* New York: Basic Books.

Mueller,C.M. & Dweck, C.S. (1998). Intelligence praise can undermine motivation and performance. *Journal of Personality and Social Psychology*, 75, pp 33–52.

Miller, E.D. (2003). Reconceptualizing the role of resiliency in coping and therapy. *Journal of Loss and Trauma*, 8, 239 – 246.

Myers, D. (1992). *The Pursuit of Happiness.* New York: Morrow.

Newsom, C., et al (2003). Changes in adolescent Response Patterns on the MMPI/ MMPI-A Across Four Decades. *Journal of Personaility Assessment*, 81: pp. 74 – 84.

Nickerson, R., (1998). Conformation Bias: A ubiquitous Phenomenon in many guises. *Review of General Psychology*, 2, pp. 175–220.

Obama, B. (2011) Fixing no child left behind. Found at; www.youtube.com/watch?v=BMCLDi0gChc

O'Connor, R. & Sheehy, N. (2000). *Understanding Suicidal Behaviour.* London: British Psychological Society.

Park, N. & Peterson, C. (2006). Character strengths and happiness among young children: Content analysis of parental descriptions. *Journal of Happiness*, Studies 7 (3), 323 -341.

Paul, A. (1999). Promotional Intelligence. The article can be found at http://www.salon.com/books/it/1999/06/28/emotional

Perkins, D. (1985). Post Primary Education has little impact on informal reasoning. *Journal of Educational Psychology* , 77 (5), pp. 562–71.

Perkins, D., Jay, E. & Tishman, S. (1993). New conceptions of thinking: from ontology to education. *Educational Psychologist*, 28 (1), pp. 67–85.

Peterson, C. & Barret, L. (1987). Explanatory style and academic performance among university freshmen, *Journal of Personality and Social Psychology* 53: pp. 603 – 7.

Peterson, C. & Seligmann, M. (2004). *Character strengths and virtues: A handbook and classification.* New York: Oxford University Press.

Peterson, C. (2000). The future of optimism. *American Psychologist* 55: pp. 44 – 55.

Phillips, M. (1998). *All Must Have Prizes*. London: Little Brown. p12.

Plato. (2000). *The Republic.* USA: New York.

Plato. (1987) 'Laches' in M. Adler (Series Ed), Great books of the western world. Vol. 7. *Plato* (J. Harward Benjamin Jowett, Trans.). Chicago: Encyclopedia Britanica.

Pollack, S. (2005). Quoted by, Ravilious, K.: *Lack of cuddles in infancy may affect development in the brain.* 22/11/05

Pricewaterhouse Coopers LLP. (2001). *Teacher Workload Study – Extracts from the Pricewaterhouse Coopers Interim Report.* UK: DfES Publications

Pricewaterhouse Coopers LLP. (2007). *Independent study into school leadership,* RB818, UK: DfES Publications.

Pury, C.L.S. & Kowalski, R. M. (2007). Human strengths, courageous actions, and general and personal courage. *Journal of Positive Psychology,* 2(2), 120 – 128.

Resnick, L. (1999). Education Week Century Series, *'Making America Smarter'* 18 (40), pp. 38 – 40.

Rhodewalt, F. (1994). Conceptions of ability, achievement goals and individual differences in self handicapping behaviour: On the application of implicit theories. *Journal of Personality,* 62, pp. 67 – 85.

Richardson, H. (2011). *Parents Invited to Rate Schools.* BBC News. 18/4/11.

Richardson, K. (1999). *The Making of Intelligence.* London: Weidenfeld and Nicholson. (The old view of intelligence is described in detail here.)

Ritchhart, R. (2002). *Intellectual Character: What It Is, Why It Matters and how to get it.* San Fransisco: Jossey-Bass.

Robbins, B. & Friedman, H. (2011) Resiliency as a virtue: Contributions from Humanistic and Positive Psychology. In *Continuity versus Creative Response to Challenge: The Primacy of Resilience and Resourcefulness in Life and Therapy.* USA: Nova Publishers.

Robinson, K. (2001). *Out of Our Minds – Learning to be Creative.* Sussex: Capstone Publishing Limited.

Robinson, K. & Aronica, L. (2009). *The Element – How finding your passion changes everything.* USA & UK: Penguin Books Ltd.

Rosenburg, M. (1965). *Society and the adolescent self-image.* Princeton, NJ: Princeton University Press.

Rosenberg, S. & Hastings, P. (2003). Microbiology and Evolution: Modulating Mutation Rates in the Wild, *Science Signaling* 300, no 5624:1382.

Rowling, J. (2008) Address to Harvard Graduates. The Fringe benefits of failure. www.ted.com/talks/lang/eng/jk_rowling_the_fringe_benefits_of_failure.html

Rozin, P. & Royzman, E. (2001). Negativity Bias, negativity dominance, and contagion. *Personality and Social Psychology Review*, 5, pp 296 – 320.

Rutter, M. (1994). Resilience: some conceptual considerations. *Contemporary Paediatrics* 11: pp. 36 – 48.

Ryan, R. & Deci, E. (1985). Self-determination Theory and the facilitation of intrinsic motivation, social development and well-being. *American Psychologist* 55: pp. 68 – 78.

Ryan, R. & Deci, E. (2000). The 'what' and 'why' of goal pursuits: Human needs and the self-determination of behavior. *Psychological Inquiry.* 11 (4), 227.

Sartor, D.C. (2003). Psychotherapy, contemplative spirituality, and the experience of Divine Mercy. *Journal of Happiness Studies*, 7. Pp377 – 395.

Scheier, M. & Carver, C. (1985). Optimism, coping and health: assessment and implications of generalized outcome expectancies. *Health Psychology*, 4: pp. 219 – 47.

Scheier, M., Carver, C. & Bridges, M. (2000). Optimism, Pessimism and Psychological Well Being. In E. Chang (ed), *Optimism and Pessimism: Theory, Research and Practice*. Washington DC: American Psychological Association.

Schulz, K. (2010). *Being Wrong, Adventures In The Margin Of Error*, USA: Portobello Books.

Schwartz, B. & Sharpe, K.E. (2005). Practical wisdom: Aristotle meets positive psychology. *Journal of Happiness Studies*, 7, pp377 – 395.

Scott, J. (2007). The Effect Of Perfectionism and Unconditional Self – Acceptance on Depression, *Journal of Rational- Emotive and Cognitive-behavior therapy* 25. No 1.

Seligmann, M. (1998). *Learned Optimism: How to Change Your Mind and Your Life*. New York: Pocket Books.

Seligman, M. (2011). *Flourish, A New Understanding of Happiness and Well-Being – and How To Achieve Them*. USA: Nicholas Brealey Publishing.

Seligmann, M. (2003). *Authentic Happiness, Using the new Positive Psychology to Realize your potential for lasting fulfillment.* UK: Nicholas Brealey Publishing. P 217.

Sheldon, K. & Elliot, A. (1999). Goal striving, need satisfaction, and longitudinal well-being: The self-concordance model. *Journal of Personality and Social Psychology*, 76, pp 482 – 497.

Slater, L. (2002). *The trouble with self-esteem.* New York Times.

Smiley, P. & Dweck, C. (1994). Individual differences in achievement goals among young children. *Child Development*, 65, pp. 1723–43.

Snyder, C. (2000). *The handbook of hope.* Orlando FL: Academic Press.

Sternberg, R. (2005) .Intelligence, Competence and Expertise, In Elliot, A. & Dweck, C., (2005) *Handbook of Competence and Motivation,* New York: Guildford Press. pp. 15 – 27.

Stewart, W. (2009). From zero to hero and back again. *The Times Education Supplement*, Section 2, Page 3. 6/4/09.

Stigler, M. (1990). *History of Statistics: The Measurement of Uncertainty Before 1900,* UK: Harvard University Press, pp 31 – 38 and 109 – 148

Stout, M. (2000). *The Feel Good Curriculum.* Cambridge MA: Perseus Books. P263.

Sykes, C. (1996). *Dumbing Down Our Kids: Why American Children Feel Good About Themselves But Can't Read, Write, or Add.* USA: St Martin's Griffin.

Taylor, C., Bandura, A., Cioffi,D., Barr, B. & Mary, E. (1988). Percieved self efficacy in coping with cognitive stressors and opioid activation. *Journal of Personality and Social Psychology.* Vol 55(3), pp. 479-488.

Taylor, S. (1989). *Positive Illusions: Creative self–deception and the Healthy Mind.* New York: Basic Books.

Taylor, S. & Brown, J. (1988). Illusion and well being: a social- psychological perspective on mental health. *Psychological Bulletin* 103: pp. 193 – 210.

Taylor, S. & Brown, J. (1994). Positive Illusions and well- being revisited: separating fact from fiction. *Psychological Bulletin* 116: pp. 21 – 7.

Tavris, C. & Aronson, E. (2008). *Mistakes Were Made (But not by me)*. UK: Pinter and Martin Ltd.

Tesser, A. (2000). On the confluence of self-esteem maintenance mechanisms. *Personality and Social Psychology Review*, 4, pp. 290 – 299.

Tetlock, P. (1985). Accountability: a social check on the fundamental attribution error, *Social Psychology Quarterly*, 48 (3) pp. 227 – 36.

The Independent Newspaper. (2006). Illiterate pupils cost £10 billion a year, warn business. 21/08/06 in, Claxton, G. (2008) *What's the Point of School?*, UK: Oneworld Publications.

The Times Educational Supplement. (2006). Maths Dumbded down at GCSE, 24/2/06. In, Claxton, G. (2008) *What's the Point of School?*. UK: Oneworld Publications.

The Times Education Supplement. (2006). One in six admit to cheating, 17/3/06 F, Furedi. In, Claxton, G. (2008) *What's the Point of School?*, UK: Oneworld Publications.

The Times Education Supplement. (2006). *Test Chief's reject plan to spot A Level stars* at 11, 3/3/06

The Times Educational Supplement. (2006). Testing dumbes down learning, 24/2/06 D, Williams. In, Claxton, G. (2008) *What's the Point of School?*, UK: Oneworld Publications.

The Guardian. (2006). What's Wrong With Cheats? 28/3/06. Furedi, F. in Claxton, G. (2008) *What's the Point of School?*, UK: Oneworld Publications.

The Guardian. (2007). Mc Culloch, A. *British Children Poorer, at greater risk and more insecure. 15/2/2007.*

The Guardian. (2004). *New Economics Foundation* report. 27/4/07

The Observer. (2006) Boston, K. *Exam strain on schools too great, 26/32006*

Thurman, R.A.E. (2005). A Buddhist view of the skill of happiness. *Advances in Mind-Body Medicine*, 21 (3-4), 29 - 32

Tiger, L. (1979). *Optimism: the biology of hope.* New York: Simon and Schuster.

Twenge, J. (2006). *Generation Me.* New York: Free Press, a division of Simon and Schuster Inc.

Vonnegut, K. (1992). *Mother Night.* New York: Vintage.

Weare, K. (2004). *Developing the Emotionally Literate School*, London: Paul Chapman Publishing.

Weare, K. & Gray, G. (2003). *What works in developing children's emotional and social competence and well-being?* University of Southampton: Department for Education and Skills Publications, Research Report 456, pp 5 – 7.

Wegela, K.K. (2009*). The courage to be present: Buddhism, psychotherapy, and the awakening of natural wisdom.* Boston, MA: Shambhala Publications.

Weinberg, D. et al, (2007) Journal of Cognitive Neuroscience, reviewed in *The Psychologist*, 20 (8), p. 461.

Weick, K. (2006). The Role of Values In High Risk Organizations. In E. Hess and K. Cameron (Eds), *Leading With Values: Positivity, Virtue and High Performance.* Cambridge: Cambridge University Press.

Weick, K. & Sutcliffe, K. (2007). *Managing the Unexpected: Resilient Performance in an Age of Uncertainty.* San Fransisco: Jossey–Bass.

Western, D., Kilts, C., *et al* (2006). The Neural Basis of Motivated Reasoning: An fMRI Study of Emotional Constraints on Political Judgment During the US Presidential Election of 2004. *Journal of Cognitive Neuroscience* 18, pp. 1947 – 1958.

William, D. (2007). Content then process: teacher learning communities in the service of formative assessment. In D.B Reeves (ed) *Ahead of the curve: The power of assessment to transform teaching and learning.* Solution Tree: Bloomington, IN pp. 183 – 204, 97.

Winograd, E. & Neisser, U. (1991). *Phantom Flashbulbs: False Recollections of Hearing the News about Challenger, affect and accuracy in recall*, Cambridge university press 9 – 31 (More detail can be found in Schulz, K. (2010) *Being Wrong, Adventures In The Margin Of Error*, UK: Portobello Books. P355)

White, J. (2006). *Intelligence, Destiny and Education*. London: Routledge.

Wood, J. (1996). What is social comparison and how should we study it? *Personality and Social Psychology Bulletin*, 22: pp. 520 -37.

Yankelovich, D. & Furth, I. (2005). The Role of Colleges in an Era of Mistrust. *The Chronicle of Higher Education*, pp. B8 – B11.

Zahavi. A. & Zahavi, A. (1997). *The Handicap Principle*. New York: Oxford University Press.

Positive Failure

Index